MILK TRAINS
AND TRAFFIC

Jeff Wilson

Kalmbach
Media

On the cover: Workers transfer milk between a Borden "butter dish" tank car and a tank trailer in New York City in 1940 (top). *New York Central*; Bottom, from left: A Supplee milk tank car behind a Huntington & Broad Top locomotive, *Al Rung*; Workers load a refrigerator car with butter at the Land O'Lakes plant in Minneapolis, *John Vachon, Library of Congress*; A worker unloads a milk can car, *U.S. Department of Agriculture*

Facing page: An Erie PA leads a westbound train with several milk and express cars in the late 1940s. *Trains magazine collection*

Back cover, from left: Empty milk and cream cans are loaded aboard a Denver & Rio Grande Western baggage car at Montrose, Colo., in 1940. *Russell Lee, Library of Congress*; A pair of bell-shaped Borden containers on a National Car Co. flatcar are tucked behind the Rutland engine at Alburgh, Vt., in October 1951. *Jim Shaughnessy*

Kalmbach Media
21027 Crossroads Circle
Waukesha, Wisconsin 53186
www.KalmbachHobbyStore.com

Published in 2019
23 22 21 20 19   1 2 3 4 5

Manufactured in China

ISBN: 978-1-62700-696-5
EISBN: 978-1-62700-697-2

Editor: Eric White
Book Design: Lisa Schroeder

Library of Congress Control Number: 2018967289

Contents

Introduction

As American cities grew larger in the 1800s, the demand for fresh milk grew with them. Milk is an extremely perishable product—it can spoil within hours if not kept at a low temperature, and its lifespan isn't long even when kept cold. Milk was also extremely susceptible to contamination from handling, especially in the early days of hand milking and before pasteurization and modern bottling processes were developed.

Although some cows were kept in large cities, the lack of grazing fields and the low-quality feed they were given (often spent mash from breweries) resulted in "swill milk," which had an off taste and odor—and that was even when it was fresh. Customers much preferred "country milk" from cows grazed on grass in pastures.

The challenge in the early 1800s was transporting fresh milk quickly from outlying areas to the city. It was nearly impossible with horse-and-wagon transport, which is why much early milk was processed into butter and cheese. However, as railroads began expanding their routes in the mid-1800s, milk became a key traffic source for Northeastern railroads.

Cows produce milk every day. Unlike factories where production can be slowed or stopped, a dairy farm produces a set amount of milk each day. This, with a highly perishable product, demanded fast, regular, efficient rail service.

By the late 1800s a traffic pattern had developed. Farmers in rural areas delivered their milk each morning to collection stations and creameries in small towns. Railroads then gathered this milk and delivered it to processing plants in larger cities. Carrying this traffic in passenger trains provided the speed needed, enabling milk collected one morning to be bottled and loaded aboard wagons and trucks for delivery to homes in cities hundreds of miles distant the next morning.

By 1900, milk was traveling up to 500 miles by rail each day in this fashion. Large-scale operations were concentrated in the Northeast, with Boston, New York, and Philadelphia the major centers. Chicago also hosted significant milk traffic by rail.

Many routes—especially into New York and Boston—justified entire trains of milk cars, with the New York Central; Erie; Delaware, Lackawanna & Western; and others running multiple milk trains.

A Rutland milk extra switches cars at Leicester Junction, Vt., in August 1946. Two General American milk tank cars trail the 2-8-0. *J.P. Ahrens*

Railroads that carried a lot of milk invested in specialized cars for the traffic. Initially this meant "can cars" to carry the 40-gallon milk cans that became icons of the dairy industry. These cars were distinctive for each railroad. The 1920s saw the development of bulk milk tank cars. These, which looked like express refrigerators, had glass-lined tanks enclosed in a carbody. Tank cars took over most milk traffic, although some was still carried in cans until the demise of milk trains.

In many areas of the country where there wasn't enough milk traffic to warrant specialized cars, milk cans were still carried as express aboard baggage cars. Farmers would get their milk cans to the local depot, where they would be loaded aboard baggage-express cars and taken to creameries in nearby towns or cities.

Rail milk traffic remained significant into the 1930s. As with other types of short-haul traffic, trucks began taking away a growing percentage of milk shipments as highways improved and trucks became larger and faster. Railroad milk traffic peaked in 1931 and soon began dropping. The Depression was a major factor, as was the demise of many passenger trains and routes following World War II. Rail milk traffic continued to decline through the 1940s. Although some traffic lasted through the 1960s, most was gone by the late 1950s.

Modeling

Milk traffic offers many possibilities for model railroaders, whether you're interested in large operations (such as the multiple solid milk trains of the New York Central) or smaller operations like the Rutland or Central Vermont.

There are many modeling options, including re-creating the many styles of small collection stations, creameries, and milk platforms located in hundreds of small towns along rail lines. You could also model a large-city milk platform where milk trains terminated and transferred their loads to trucks for the final few miles to processing creameries.

Operations offer great variety as well. You can replicate the trains that pick up can or bulk cars at multiple creameries and towns, the switching operations where cars and cans are combined and sorted for delivery to multiple destinations, or run solid milk trains on priority schedules to large-city terminals. Even in areas not considered milk runs, cans were collected as express, so you can show these cans on station platforms and have passenger trains load them at their stops.

Models of various creameries and milk platforms have been produced by many manufacturers, including American Model Builders, BTS, Deerfield River Laser, JL Innovative Design, Laser Art Structures, ModelTech Studios, The N Scale Architect, and Walthers. Milk cars have been

One of Borden's distinctive "butter-dish" milk tank cars is loaded at a small-town creamery in the late 1940s. *New York Central*

made by Athearn, InterMountain, and Walthers, and cast-resin kits for many specialty milk cars have been offered by Funaro & Camerlengo.

Whichever modeling and operating options you choose, if you model the steam era through the 1950s (and in some areas even later) you have opportunities to add facets of the milk and dairy industry to your model railroad.

Turn the page and we'll start with a look at the history of the dairy industry itself, then see how railroads became key components of the process of getting milk from outlying farms to customers in large and small cities.

1

CHAPTER ONE

History of milk and dairy operations

Many railroads operated solid trains of milk cars or trains that were mainly milk with a coach or two at the rear. Erie train No. 9 totes a string of empty milk cars near Lanesboro Junction, Pa., in the 1940s. They're on their way toward Elmira for reloading at various local creameries along the line. Two of Borden's distinctive "butter dish" tank cars are in the consist. *Wayne Brumbaugh*

Milk was an important, high-priority traffic source for many railroads into the 1950s. Railroads carried milk from creameries and small collection stations in rural areas to bottling and processing plants in large cities. In some areas, especially in the Northeast, this was done by dedicated trains, **1**. In addition, railroads carried—and still carry—finished dairy products, namely butter, condensed and powdered milk, and cheese.

Railroads' milk business emerged and grew in the mid- to late 1800s with the expansion of rail lines, the growth of dairy farms, and the shift of farming from subsistence to revenue-producing. This was driven by the population growth of large cities—and the resulting demand for larger quantities of milk—and the evolution of technology in both farming and creamery operations.

It was the emergence of railroads that allowed dairy operations to move toward commercial large-scale production by expanding potential markets beyond the nearest small towns. The first regular shipment of milk by rail took place in 1842, when Erie predecessor New York & Erie carried loads of raw milk from near Chester, N.Y. (Orange County), to New York City. The distance was only about 50 miles, but in that era the distance represented a significant challenge for a perishable product.

The public's reception to the high quality of this "country" milk over the "swill milk" produced in the city was positive, and demand grew rapidly. Rail operations to bring milk to large cities soon expanded both in number of routes as well as length of travel.

Rail milk operations were common to New England and the Northeast, with solid trains of milk cars heading to Boston, New York, and Philadelphia on several railroads, including the Boston & Maine, **2**; Delaware, Lackawanna & Western; Erie; New York Central; New York, New Haven & Hartford; New York, Ontario & Western; Pennsylvania; and others.

Milk traffic by rail was not confined to that region. Chicago hosted a sizable amount of rail-based milk operations into the 1940s, with feeder lines extending throughout northern Illinois and much of Wisconsin as well as parts of Indiana on routes of the Chicago & North Western, Soo Line (the original Wisconsin Central), and six other railroads.

Across much of the rest of the country, railroads carried smaller—but still significant—amounts of milk in cans as LCL (less-than-carload) or in passenger-train baggage cars as express (by Railway Express Agency, REA), **3**.

Most milk cars traveled as head-end traffic on passenger trains, or by themselves as a dedicated train, where traffic warranted. Pairing milk with passenger trains provided regular schedules and the speed required to get the product to market in a timely manner, something that was just not possible with freight-train schedules. The phrase "milk run" refers to the early milk trains: meaning a regular train that stops at almost every station to gather cans.

As with many other time-sensitive commodities, trucks began taking a significant amount of milk business from railroads starting in the 1920s, starting with shorter routes (up to 50 and even 100 miles). Cities located in or near agricultural areas were soon receiving most of their milk by truck. Detroit, for example, went from receiving 84 percent of its milk by rail in 1915 (much via electric railways) to just 12 percent by 1924. Minneapolis and St. Paul, in the heart of the Midwestern dairy belt, received just 6 percent of milk by rail by 1924.

As highways continued improving and trucks became larger, railroads

Cow terminology

There are several terms for livestock: A milch cow is a cow in milk or kept primarily for milk. A heifer is a young female that has not yet had a calf; a cow is a mature female that has calved at least once. A steer is a neutered male, and a bull is an adult male. Bulls were kept for breeding, while steers were usually fed and kept for eventual sale or slaughter.

Diesels headed many milk trains from the 1940s onward. An A-B set of EMD F3s leads Boston & Maine train 5507, bringing empty milk cars northward near Fitchburg, Mass., in 1952. *George C. Corey*

couldn't compete even on longer hauls, and the amount of milk carried began declining on most routes from the 1930s onward. Even rail traffic to Boston and New York, which received milk from up to 400 and 500 miles distant, began a steady decline. The elimination of many passenger trains and routes after World War II was a contributing factor as well. Some milk business lasted through the 1960s, with the Boston & Maine carrying the last raw milk shipments by rail in 1972.

Although the era of the milk train has long passed, the business provided more than 100 years of traffic for railroads. The trains, railcars, creameries, operations, and myriad details are fascinating and present many opportunities for modeling. The potentials are broad: from a small-town creamery shipping a can car of milk or a refrigerator car of butter, to a large-city milk terminal with dozens of trucks lining up to off-load cans or transload bulk milk from cars to trucks, **4**.

A review of the history of the dairy industry will help better understand railroads' roles in handling the business, how it grew and declined, and show how finished-product traffic continues.

Early milk and dairy history

Milk has been a key part of diets in many cultures for thousands of years. Humans first began getting milk from animals around 8000 B.C., and shortly thereafter were making cheese and butter—both of which last much longer than unrefrigerated raw milk, which must be consumed shortly after it is obtained.

Cheese was produced locally wherever there was a supply of milk. Cheese is made in thousands of varieties, all with different attributes, from fancy to plain. Cheese was often used as payment or barter. Parmesan was a well-known luxury item by the 1300s, and more common varieties of cheese were a staple food for many. Cheese was also one of the foods carried on long voyages, including naval and commercial ships, and used in hospitals and other institutions. Cheese has long been known as "everyone's food."

3

By the 1670s, the city of Gouda (Netherlands) was marketing more than 6 million pounds of cheese per year. The Dutch were leaders in milk production, and worked to find ways of increasing milk output from cows. They were among the first to make dairy farming a business, and in nearby cities they found ready markets for their products. By 1700, some cows were producing more than 300 gallons (2,400 pounds) of milk (double that of a cow in 14th century England).

Cattle were brought to North America beginning in the 1600s, and they were highly valued. Cattle in Colonial times served multiple purposes. The males were used to work fields and do labor; females produced calves each year and also provided milk. Cattle were a symbol of wealth—

they were, in effect, currency, and could be traded and sold readily, while at the same time providing income and easing labor.

Many of the Europeans who settled in the U.S. were farmers (especially English, Dutch, and Swedes), and they continued working to develop positive traits in their livestock, including as milk/dairy providers. This, however, took time, and was largely dependent upon advances in transportation.

In Colonial times in the U.S., milk wasn't widely accepted as a key food item—it was more of a benefit of having animals around. This changed and evolved as more settlers arrived and cities began to grow. One author described the transformation as "dietary opportunism."

Farming at the time was much

Although the Burlington didn't operate dedicated milk trains into Lincoln, Neb., signs of heavy milk traffic are seen with cans on numerous carts as well as on a platform—with what appear to be a pair of milk cars—at left. *J. Young; collection of Jim Seacrest*

different than today. With little mechanization and horse-drawn equipment, most farms were small operations. Most farms were subsistence operations—growing crops and keeping various animals on hand—and most had a dairy cow or two. Milking was done by hand in the morning and evening.

Milk had to be consumed the day of production or immediately turned into butter and cheese. Although butter and cheese had longer shelf lives, the lack of refrigeration and the difficulty of long-distance travel were impediments to selling the products.

Railroads began changing that by the mid-1800s. Along with milk going to big cities, butter also found a ready market. By the 1850s, carloads of butter were traveling from Vermont to New York City. The first creameries and cheese factories began to appear, where production could be done on a larger scale using milk from multiple farms.

The growth of railroads and the development of creameries meant larger farms and more specialization by the late 1800s. Some farms began to specialize in dairy operations, evolving from making small batches of butter and cheese to concentrating on becoming specialists in producing milk—leaving the production and marketing of milk products to others.

Larger dairy herds meant more work, with two-a-day milkings done by hand (along with all of the other work needed on a farm), **5**. Not only was this time-consuming, it wasn't always a clean process, with an open pail under the cow.

This milk was poured through a strainer into a milk can. Cans from the evening milking were placed in a cooling tank, **6**, to keep milk (preferably below 50 degrees) until morning. Some farms had well or spring water that was cool enough; farmers sometimes had to buy ice to keep the tank cool in warm weather. Milk from evening and morning milkings were brought to market (creamery or rail station) first thing in the morning.

Many attempts were made to mechanize the milking process, but a

Milk was transloaded to trucks at many big-city terminals for movement to off-line processing plants. This is New York state Dairy Queen Beverly Prior watching as Dairylea milk is transferred at New York Central's 60th Street Yard in July 1951. *New York Central*

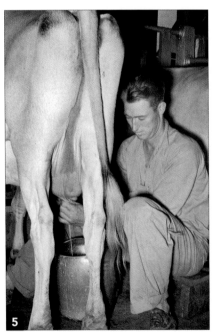

Milking by hand was the only option into the 1890s. It was time-consuming, and the open bucket left many chances for contamination. *Russell Lee, Library of Congress*

lack of electricity in most rural areas limited the options. The first successful device was the Mehring milking machine, introduced in 1892. It was powered by foot pedals and allowed milking two cows at once with the operator sitting between, **7**. It was made through 1920, with more than 3,000 sold. Another early machine was the "Thistle" milker, which used a vacuum pump driven by steam. It was efficient, didn't require manpower (like the Mehring), but was difficult to keep clean and required a steam source.

By the 1920s and '30s, electricity was available in more rural areas. The real innovation came in 1922 with the Surge milking machine. It was electrically powered, used pulsating movement, and fed milk into a small enclosed container that was suspended under the cow (a simple harness went over the cow's back). This was important to keep milk clean. It quickly became the preferred method

for larger dairy operations, **8**.

The number of cows in the U.S. grew dramatically, from 26 million in 1860 to 52 million in 1900. Not only were the number of farms and size of herds increasing, but dairy operations were spreading westward as well. The charts in **9** show where the key dairy regions were in 1880 and 1920 (note that the map features only those cows kept primarily for milk production, not all cows).

Developing markets

Creameries began appearing in small towns and cities by the 1860s. Most of these creameries served as collection points for farmers, where milk was consolidated for shipment to processing and bottling plants in larger cities. This became the largest market for finished products in the biggest metro areas. Other creameries processed the raw milk into butter and cheese, which was also marketed in large areas.

The good news for farmers was that they now had a ready, consistent market for their product. Through the late 1800s, farmers sold their milk based on volume. A problem was that there was no bonus for quality: Some farmers illicitly added water to milk to increase volume—a tactic that was difficult to catch—or simply sold poor-quality milk that had less butterfat.

The solution came in 1890 when Stephen Babcock developed what become known as the Babcock Test as a simple way to measure butterfat content in milk, **10**. It involves adding to a sample of milk a specific amount of sulfuric acid, which dissolves everything but the butterfat, then heating the mix and separating out the fat with a centrifuge.

The test was accurate, quick to perform, and gave a benchmark for milk quality. It was soon in practice on farms and at every creamery and milk depot in the country. Raw milk was soon being sold by weight (by hundredweight, or 100 pounds), usually with adjustments for specific butterfat content.

Selling to consumers was another story. Door-to-door milk sales were common in large cities by the 1800s—about the only option since stores didn't have refrigeration to keep milk fresh. In some cases a cow was led around and milked as needed when

Dairy breeds

Four cattle breeds came to dominate milk production in the U.S.: the Holstein, Jersey, Guernsey, and Brown Swiss, with smaller numbers of Ayrshire and Milking Shorthorn cows. The Holstein is by far the dominant breed, currently making up 85 percent of cows in production. The familiar black-and-white—sometimes red-and-white—cow became popular for one main reason: higher production than other breeds, even though they produce milk with less milkfat (about 3.5 percent) compared to other breeds. They readily adapt to various situations and areas, whether grazing or on feed, and—a key in the 1800s—Holsteins produce well even when food resources are limited.

The breed originated in the Netherlands but were brought to the U.S. relatively late, in the 1850s. A grown Holstein cow weighs an average of 1,300 pounds, and today will produce about 22,000 pounds of milk per year, and have a productive milking span of about six years.

The second most-common breed in the U.S., the Jersey, accounts for just over 8 percent of total milk cows. Jerseys are the common "brown cow," but some are brown and white, with a black nose and white muzzle. They are smaller than Holsteins (about 1,000 pounds) and typically produce less milk (about 16,500 pounds annually) but Jersey milk is well-regarded for its higher milkfat content (25 percent higher than average) and protein content, making the breed popular among cheese and butter producers. Jersey farmers also claim that milk from Jerseys is the best-tasting.

Jerseys are known for being efficient at grazing and feeding. Since they weigh about 25 percent less than a Holstein, they also eat less. They also have longer production periods and lifespans, and cows produce more calves on average than Holsteins. The breed doesn't take its name from the state—instead they are named for Jersey Island (off the coast of France). They are among the oldest cattle breeds, brought to the U.S. in the 1850s.

Guernseys make up about 1.3 percent of U.S. dairy herds,. The breed originated in the United Kingdom by the late 1700s, and they first came to the U.S. in 1840. Guernseys are reddish to brown, often with clearly defined white patches. A Guernsey cow weighs about 1,100 pounds and produces about 16,500 pounds of milk per year. Guernseys are known for being efficient, requiring less feed to produce the same amount of milk as other breeds, with higher butterfat content and protein compared to Holsteins. Their milk is typically slightly golden white (giving them the "golden Guernsey" nickname which was also adopted as a brand name for many years).

Brown Swiss are not as common, comprising less than 1 percent of U.S. herds. They are brown with distinctive large, "fluffy" ears, and are among the world's oldest dairy cattle breeds, originating in the Swiss Alps several centuries ago. Brown Swiss tend to be larger than other breeds—about 1,500 pounds—with strong, tall bodies, and are resilient to weather and land conditions. They have good production (about 18,500 pounds per year), with longer production lives than Holsteins. They are favored by cheesemakers for their high protein content and close fat-to-protein ratio. They were first brought to U.S. in 1869, imported from Switzerland.

Holstein

Jersey

Guernsey

a customer wanted milk. Another method was for a farmer to bring cans on a wagon, and ladle the customer's purchase directly from the can. This presented several challenges, namely making sure the milk didn't turn sour in the time from milking to delivery. Customers also had to trust the seller that the milk hadn't been sitting in the sun for hours or was watered down—an all-too-common tactic of farmers to extend the product.

Some cows were kept in large cities. The lack of grazing area meant they had to be fed, usually with the cheapest feed possible. This usually meant spent mash and grain from beer and other alcohol production. Combined with crowed, poor conditions in most city animal stalls, the result was milk that usually had an off taste and color. It was usually referred to as "swill milk."

Getting country milk to the city soon became a priority. Early rail transport to cities resulted in milk depots, where milk was offloaded and sold directly to consumers—ladling into their own containers. Moving to the next step—bottled and packaged products—meant solving challenges in milk quality, refrigeration, packaging, transportation, and other issues.

Cans from the evening milking were placed in cooling tanks. Running water from a spring or well was sometimes sufficient to keep milk cool. *Russell Lee, Library of Congress*

Pasteurization and milk purity

The major challenge was that raw milk has an extremely short shelf life, even if cooled. It would go sour within a day if not cooled. Raw milk can also be contaminated in many ways, starting with unhealthy cows and including improper handling at milking or any intermediate step. By the late 1800s, scientists understood that microbes and contamination by manure during milking, as well as other post-milking contamination by improper handling, could lead to many diseases including cholera, foot-and-mouth disease, tuberculosis, scarlet fever, diphtheria, and typhoid.

Unless you were getting milk directly from the cow, raw milk was—although valued—a suspect product.

Adding to the general worries about milk quality was the infant mortality rate, which was high, especially in

The Mehring milking machine, powered by foot pedals, was among the earliest successful milking devices. It allowed milking two cows at once. More than 3,000 were made from 1892 to 1920. *U.S. Department of Agriculture*

large cities. Surveys discovered that babies consuming cow's milk had a notably higher rate of sickness and death—especially in summer months—compared to those who were breast-fed. This caused groups to focus attention on improving milk quality: the "milk reform" of the 1890s.

It was largely consumer groups working for safer milk that eventually brought about reform—not government regulations. Higher-grade and/or pasteurized or sterilized milk was available in many areas, but at a much higher price. Moves to require all milk to meet high standards were met with resistance from producers. This was especially true of small operations, where individual farmers marketed to their own customers, or small dealers that didn't have the money for equipment or testing. Also, few animals were being tested for diseases.

The breakthrough to increasing milk's shelf life and improving safety was pasteurization. Louis Pasteur himself had been more concerned with wine and beer, not milk, but the method was readily adapted to milk. Pasteurization is the process of heating milk for a short period of time, then rapidly cooling it. This killed microbes and kept milk from spoiling, making it safer and greatly improving its shelf life.

The process was first done with milk in the 1880s, but pasteurization was not immediately widely adopted. Many producers were reluctant, as the required equipment and process represented added expenses. And despite scientists' and doctors' assurances that the process worked, there was much skepticism among consumers as well as many in the health field. Claims ranged from those who thought treated milk tasted different to those who claimed the process was a hoax to increase prices.

Some cities and state agencies began requiring that commercial milk be pasteurized just after the turn of the century. Chicago adopted a partial pasteurization law in 1908, Minnesota in 1909; New York City enacted a law in 1909 and required pasteurization by

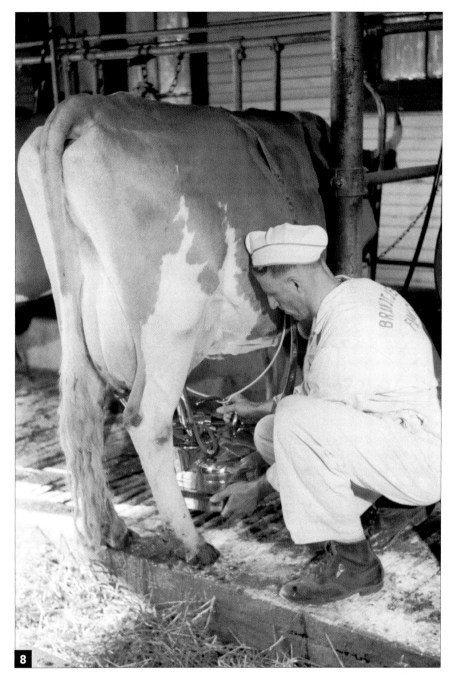

8

The electrically powered Surge milking machine made large dairy herds possible. It used pulsating movement with an enclosed container suspended under the cow.
Arthur Rothstein, Library of Congress

1916, and Massachusetts in 1914.

As late as 1920, a Milwaukee ordinance requiring pasteurization was challenged by city milk dealers on the grounds that it would hurt business and did not promote public health. It took a state Supreme Court ruling to uphold the law in 1920, with the court finding that "public health demands that milk and all milk products should be pure and wholesome," citing scientific proof of the process.

Bottling and processing

Milk, even after being properly pasteurized, was sometimes contaminated or mishandled by allowing it to remain warm for too long, by placing it in contaminated bottles, by unclean piping or handling equipment, or by not refrigerating it at a low enough temperature after packaging (including by dealers after distribution, or at stores with improper coolers).

Bottling milk was a step forward

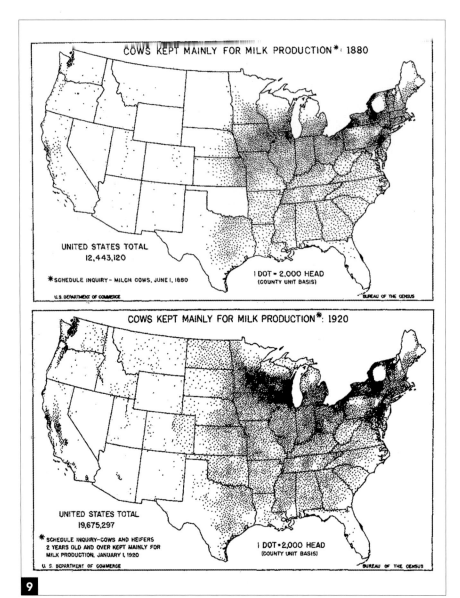

COWS KEPT MAINLY FOR MILK PRODUCTION*: 1880

UNITED STATES TOTAL
12,443,120

* SCHEDULE INQUIRY - MILCH COWS, JUNE 1, 1880

1 DOT = 2,000 HEAD
(COUNTY UNIT BASIS)

U.S. DEPARTMENT OF COMMERCE

BUREAU OF THE CENSUS

COWS KEPT MAINLY FOR MILK PRODUCTION*: 1920

UNITED STATES TOTAL
19,675,297

* SCHEDULE INQUIRY-COWS AND HEIFERS
2 YEARS OLD AND OVER KEPT MAINLY FOR
MILK PRODUCTION, JANUARY 1, 1920

U.S. DEPARTMENT OF COMMERCE

1 DOT = 2,000 HEAD
(COUNTY UNIT BASIS)

BUREAU OF THE CENSUS

9

These maps show key areas of dairy herds in 1880 and 1920. Most dairy production is centered in the Northeast and Midwest. *U.S. Department of Agriculture*

compared to "loose milk," **11**. Bottling began in the late 1880s, but the new technology presented some challenges. Investing in the bottles themselves, as well as the filling equipment, represented a significant expense for producers. Selling was another challenge, as stores typically didn't have refrigerated or iced coolers to store the product. Yet another problem was dealing with the returned bottles. Users were supposed to clean the bottles before returning them, but that was a dicey proposition.

However, bottling technology improved, and producers began investing in better equipment. By the 1910s most large plants were using rotary bottling machines that both filled and capped bottles quickly, and more importantly, they were using automated cleaning and sterilizing equipment for incoming empty bottles. Mechanical refrigeration was becoming the norm, eliminating many issues with souring milk.

All of this led to safer, more-consistent quality of milk, and sales kept increasing. The public push for safe milk had continued, and knowledge of nutrition and the discovery of vitamins increased the status of milk as a healthy part of a diet—something milk producers pushed in their advertisements and marketing campaigns.

Homogenized milk was the next development in processing. Through the 1920s, if you bought a quart bottle of milk and let it stand, the cream would rise to the top in a visible layer. Homogenizing was the process of breaking down the milk fat globules so they stay mixed within the milk instead of rising to and floating on the surface.

The process met resistance among consumers, who were used to seeing the cream in their milk. Although homogenized milk began appearing in the 1920s, it didn't become common until after World War II.

Dairy producers favored homogenized milk, because it allowed them to remove the cream and then blend it back with the milk in precise percentages, with the excess cream going to other uses. The result became whole milk, with an industry standard of 3.25 percent fat (or 3.5, depending upon local regulations); and two-percent milk. Skim milk (all fat removed, with about .1 percent residual), originally called "skimmed milk" because all of the cream was skimmed from it, was originally a byproduct, and through the 1930s was primarily used as animal feed supplement or in chocolate making or other food processing.

The lack of refrigeration in stores and homes (and limited space in home iceboxes) made daily door-to-door milk delivery a standard service in most cities and large towns. Dairies had fleets of delivery wagons and trucks to get their products directly to homes, **12**. As late as the 1950s, 70 percent of homes received milk this way, but as refrigerators replaced iceboxes in homes and supermarkets and stores began selling more milk, home delivery dropped dramatically.

Depression and recovery

Early Depression years were hard on the milk industry and other food producers, with a glut of many food products—something that had never happened before—and consumers turning to less-expensive foods. This led to the government stepping in to guide dairy prices.

The dairy industry has always been

plagued by dramatic price swings, caused by many factors including competition among competing cooperatives, alleged price fixing by large dairy companies, and seasonal production swings (more milk in spring, less in fall). The core problem is that farmers have a daily production that must be sold; it can't simply be stored like grain. Farmers can't simply produce less milk if prices drop or more milk if demand increases—they're tied to their herds.

As the Depression started, demand dropped, and producers lobbied for the government to regulate prices. This initially resulted in the Agricultural Adjustment Act of 1933, which led to raising and leveling prices for milk and other agricultural products. It was eventually struck down by the Supreme Court, but a revised version, the Agricultural Marketing Agreement Act of 1937, took over. The goal was to ensure an adequate milk supply while providing a fair price for producers. It sets a minimum price that processors must pay to farmers and cooperatives (which is adjusted by region and is based mainly on supply and demand, not the cost of production).

Part of this was the government buying excess milk and providing it free or at reduced cost to children in schools across the country (followed by subsidized lunches, through the National School Lunch Act in 1946). This did double duty, providing nutritious meals to children in need and providing a ready market for milk.

Many small creameries did not survive the Depression. In many regions, there were fewer than half the creameries in 1940 as in the late 1920s. As demand increased again in the 1940s, surviving creameries continued to grow and improve efficiency. Dairy herds, which had shrunk in the 1930s, also began expanding as electricity came to most rural areas, with milking machines and bulk tanks made processes more efficient.

Butter and other milk products

Along with market milk (milk intended for resale as such), a great

Milk and Dairy Timeline

1611—First cows arrive in North America, to Jamestown Colony
1842—First regular shipment of milk by rail (Orange County to New York City)
1851—First wholesale ice-cream plant (Baltimore; owned by Jacob Fussell)
1856—First patent for condensed milk (Borden's); production began in 1857
1856—First commercial butter factory
1884—Milk bottle first appears
1886—Automatic bottling/capping machine appears
1888—First dedicated milk railcars placed in service (Boston & Maine)
1895—First pasteurization of commercial milk
1903—Modern milking machine introduced by Alexander Gillies
1905—First milk-drying plant opens (Fayatteville, N.Y.)
1908—Chicago adopts first pasteurization law
1911—Rotary bottle filling/capping machine speeds operation
1914—First bulk (tank) trucks for milk
1919—First homogenized milk sold commercially (in Connecticut)
1920—5 million dairy farms in U.S.; 55,000 milking machines
1922—First production bulk (tank) railcars placed in service
1930—93 percent of milk into Boston arrives by rail
1930—13 percent of U.S. farms have electricity
1931—Milk rail traffic peaks
1932—Cardboard (coated) milk cartons introduced
1935—Borden's "butter dish" tank cars first appear
1936—Flatcars with detachable milk tanks begin appearing
1938—Bulk tanks began appearing at farms, replacing cans
1940—70 percent of milk is home-delivered
1944—4.5 million dairy farms; 685,000 milking machines
1946—Truman signs National School Lunch Act
1948—Ultra-high-temperature pasteurization begins
1948—Paper milk cartons begin appearing
1964—Plastic milk bottles begin appearing
1972—Last rail milk operation (on Boston & Maine into Boston)

10

The Babcock test was developed in the 1890s. It is a simple, accurate method of measuring butterfat content by adding sulfuric acid to a milk sample. *Russell Lee, Library of Congress*

15

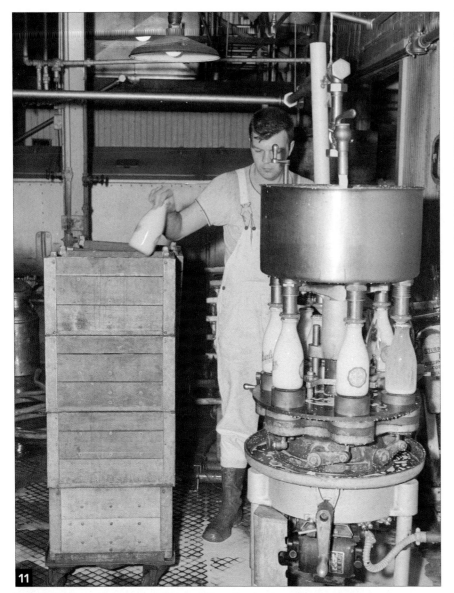

11

Pasteurization and rotary bottling machines (and automatic cappers) helped ensure the safety of market milk. This is in Burlington, Vt., in 1941. *Jack Delano, Library of Congress*

Whole milk sold by state

(states with at least 100 million gallons sold)

State	1929	1939
	(hundreds of millions)	
Wisconsin	8.3	10.1
New York	6.8	7.3
Pennsylvania	3.7	4.0
California	3.1	3.7
Illinois	2.3	3.0
Ohio	2.2	3.0
Michigan	2.2	2.8
Indiana	1.3	1.8
Vermont	1.1	1.2
Minnesota	0.9	1.2
Texas	0.7	1.2
Washington	0.9	1.1

Source: U.S. Department of Agriculture

deal of milk went to produce other products, namely butter and cheese. Dried milk, evaporated milk, and condensed milk also became common products.

As noted earlier, butter and cheese plants began appearing in the 1850s as a way to extend the life of milk. Although much of this was made in the Northeast and New England through the 1800s, the increasing demand for milk from New York, Boston, Philadelphia, and other large cities led to more milk being sold as market milk.

The result was that as dairy farms expanded through the Midwest, that area began producing the majority of the country's butter and cheese. Most was still sold in the East, but the arrangement worked well because butter and cheese were easier to ship long distances.

Among the earliest attempts to preserve milk was by evaporation. Gail Borden in the 1850s was working on ways of making preserved "portable" food. Borden borrowed ideas from others, mainly the Shakers of New York, who had successfully used a vacuum-pan method for preserving fruit. Borden applied the same methods to milk, evaporating it in a vacuum and adding sugar to preserve

it. He received huge orders for the product from the U.S. Army during the Civil War, and it continued growing in popularity into the 1900s as a recipe ingredient, coffee creamer, and for making ice cream.

A related product, evaporated milk, is similar but without the sugar added (production requires pressure cooking the cans after filling to sterilize them). It can be reconstituted into milk by adding water, and became touted as a milk substitute for infants and children and for those who don't have access to whole milk. It's also used in many recipes and as a starter for ice cream.

Yet another product is powdered milk, often made with the skim milk left over from buttermaking. It can be reconstituted as milk, and became a prime ingredient for baby food. It's also an ingredient for making chocolate in various forms, as well as various other food products. A related product is malted milk—not the ice-cream shake, but a powder made from a combination of dried milk and ground, malted grain. It was first marketed as an easy-to-digest nutritional supplement for people with indigestion, and it proved popular as a baby food and as an additive in many other foods (including milkshakes).

All of these products were shipped by rail, and although they didn't require the high speeds and coordinated schedules of milk trains, the traffic and production facilities can be fascinating to model (see more on them in Chapter 2).

Milk trains and cars

Milk was handled in baggage cars across the country and carried in specialized milk cars in several areas, but it was the Northeast that hosted the milk train, with schedules organized to get raw milk from outlying areas, **13**, to processing plants in New York, Boston, and other cities.

By the late 1800s, milk traffic had increased to the point that railroads' milk routes stretched 200 and even 300 miles from the city. By the early 1900s, some of these routes extended nearly 500 miles, requiring coordinated schedules among multiple trains and railroads, with solid trains of 20 or 30 milk cars arriving at city terminals.

Milk trains typically started their runs at outlying towns and creameries early in the morning, collecting cars and milk cans en route. Cars from multiple trains would be consolidated to larger trains, with arrival in the city in the evening or overnight. These trains sometimes had a passenger car or two, but many existed solely

Daily home milk delivery was common into the 1950s. Women took over many milk routes during World War II, as with this Supplee driver in Bryn Mawr, Pa., in 1943. *John Vachon, Library of Congress*

A Supplee milk tank car is tucked behind Huntington & Broad Top locomotive no. 2 at Saxton, Pa. It would soon be delivered to the Pennsylvania Railroad at Huntingdon, Pa., which would carry it to Philadelphia. *Al Rung*

14

Although considered passenger trains, many milk trains had just a single coach or combine at the rear, as on this Delaware, Lackawanna & Western train leaving Binghamton, N.Y., in 1937. *R.P. Morris*

to haul milk. They were typically the hottest trains on the railroad, not to be delayed, **14**.

Some large city milk plants had rail access, but most did not, requiring arriving milk (either cans or bulk loads) to be transferred to trucks for the final few miles of their journey. The milk would be quickly transferred, bottled, and ready for delivery the following morning.

By the early 1900s milk was being carried in specialized cars designed specifically for hauling milk cans, **15**. Most of these were insulated wood cars that resembled contemporary express refrigerator cars. A key difference is that most milk cars lacked the end ice bunkers of conventional refrigerator

cars. Since the milk was only on the cars for a matter of hours—instead of days, like refrigerator cars carrying, for example, produce across the country—the car's insulation (and ice shoveled atop the cans)—was sufficient to keep the load cool.

The 10-gallon can was the standard method of transporting milk into the 1920s, but they were labor-intensive to handle and clean, and it took thousands of them to do the job. Bulk milk (tank) trucks had begun appearing in the 1910s, and bulk-milk tank railcars would debut in 1922. The challenge for carrying milk had been developing a large tank or vessel that could easily be kept clean and sterile. The answer was steel tanks with an

interior glass lining. Although initially used for breweries, the technology was quickly adopted by the milk industry for both stationary tanks as well as railcars. General American paired with tank manufacturer Pfaudler to develop the most popular designs for these cars, and by the 1940s they dominated milk rail transport, **16**.

Unlike conventional railroad tank cars, most bulk milk cars had tanks inside conventional enclosed carbodies. From the outside, it's impossible to tell that inside are two insulated, glass-lined steel tanks, each holding 3,000 to 4,000 gallons of milk. The body protects the car's valves and control equipment and provides additional insulation. Bulk milk cars

15 Delaware, Lackawanna & Western No. 1635 is a 45-foot wood car for carrying milk in cans. It has high-speed trucks, passenger steam and signal lines, and inward-swinging doors. *John Nehrich collection*

16 This 40-foot steel car, built by General American-Pfaudler in the mid-1940s and leased to Borden, represents the final development in milk tank cars. It has two 3,000-gallon glass-lined tanks. *General American*

made loading and unloading faster and more efficient, doing away with the cumbersome cans. However, the bulk cars were not enough to slow the movement of milk traffic to trucks.

The final development in attempting to improve efficiency was a precursor to modern intermodal traffic, with the use of tank trailers (in piggyback fashion) and containers that could be transferred from flatcars to trucks (more on those in Chapter 4). The trailers were not successful and never got beyond experimental status, but tank containers in various styles were common sights in trains from their introduction in 1936 through the 1950s.

Demise of rail traffic

Railroad milk traffic peaked in 1931, but the coming of paved roads and

highways, larger (and more-reliable) trucks, and the time-sensitive nature of the product all led to milk traffic moving to trucks.

The demise of many passenger-train routes from the 1930s onward was another factor. As passenger trains were discontinued, railroads could no longer efficiently carry carloads of milk on the tight schedules needed. Freight trains couldn't do it, and by the 1950s few routes had enough milk traffic to justify dedicated trains. This was exacerbated by the rapid "train offs" that eliminated large numbers of passenger trains from the 1950s into the 1960s.

As an example of this shift, in 1930 Boston received 93 percent of milk by rail and 7 percent by truck; by 1940 the split had become 61 percent/39

percent and in 1955 53/47.

Some lines actively hauled milk into the 1960s, but most had shifted to trucks by the late 1950s. The last shipments—into Boston on the B&M in 1972—closed the book on a fascinating chapter in railroad history.

Even though milk itself is no longer handled by rail, a wide variety of dairy products are still carried by railroads. These are primarily the final products of creameries and processing plants, including butter and dried milk.

Turn the page and we'll take a look at the many types of creameries and dairy processing plants, see how they work and how they evolved, and see how their traffic was handled by rail.

CHAPTER TWO

Creameries and dairy processing plants

The New England Dairies facility at Enosburg Falls, Vt., on a branch of the Central Vermont, is a classic New England creamery. It's a two-story wood frame structure with a tall smokestack and covered platform, where a CV can car awaits its next load in September 1941. *Jack Delano, Library of Congress*

The word "creamery" (or "dairy") has become the generic term for almost any type of milk processing plant. These include simple early collection stations that consolidated milk to ship to larger facilities; plants that pasteurized and bottled milk and cream, **1**; and those that produce butter, evaporated and condensed milk, powdered milk, and other products.

Their sizes, how each of these operated, how they collected inbound milk, and how they shipped milk and other products evolved significantly over time. They also varied by region of the country. Railroads were heavily involved in shipping collected milk from local plants to large-city processing plants from the 1800s through the 1950s, especially in New England and the Northeast. Although that traffic has disappeared, dairy companies still ship some finished products by rail.

Creamery history

By the 1850s, farmers were making their own butter and cheese and bringing it to sell in towns and cities. Short-distance rail milk traffic had also begun, giving farmers a couple of options for making money from milk, and encouraging many to expand their dairy herds and increase production.

The natural progression was to consolidate efforts to make butter and cheese on a larger scale. History is a bit fuzzy, but credit for the first cheese factory goes to a Rome, N.Y., dairy farmer named Jesse Williams, who began making cheese using milk from multiple farms in 1851. The first creameries to make butter began appearing in 1861, and many subsequent creameries made both butter and cheese.

Initial operations were small, mainly because the cows supplying the creamery had to be nearby. In horse-and-wagon days, the maximum practical distance for carrying milk to a creamery was about 5 miles—any longer took too much time from a farmer's busy day. If the farmer separated his own cream, the distance could be longer, as cream would last longer and would only require delivery every two or three days.

This resulted in a lot of small creamery and dairy operations located in close proximity to each other. Every small town in New England and the Midwest had one or two, and some were located in the country. By the turn of the century, the U.S. Department of Agriculture (USDA) recommended that a prospective creamery should make at least 1,000 pounds of butter

The "creamery" at Erin, N.Y., on the Lehigh Valley, exemplifies the small receiving station. The turn-of-the-century view shows an open platform and the larger icehouse to the rear. *Jeff Wilson collection*

Borden had receiving stations and bottling plants in many locations. This one is at Cochecton, N.Y., on the Erie. It's a two-story wood structure with large adjoining ice house at right. *Jeff Wilson collection*

a week to be economically viable, with at least 500 nearby cows on farms supplying the business.

The coming of trucks and better roads changed the butter and cheese business dramatically, allowing raw milk to travel longer distances. By the 1910s creameries were becoming larger, a trend that would continue as small operations closed and newer, more modern plants were built. Iowa, for example, had just half the creameries

in 1921 it had in 1900, but total production had increased 40 percent. Mechanical improvements in milk handling, refrigeration, pasteurization, churning, and other production chores increased efficiency and continued through the rail-milk era.

Many small creameries were initially locally owned, but larger dairy companies gradually bought many small creameries and bottling plants. The sidebar on page 25 lists some of

The United Farmers Cooperative creamery, on the Central Vermont in East Berkshire, Vt., had a modern appearance in 1941. Cans were off-loaded from trucks on the upper level and railcars were loaded below (at right). *Jack Delano, Library of Congress*

the major dairy companies through the rail-milk era. Creameries could be privately owned or operated as cooperatives, where farmers grouped together to share expenses and profits (see "Cooperatives vs. proprietary creameries" on page 27).

Let's take a look at the various types of creameries and dairy production plants.

Collection stations

As railroads expanded their lines, a great deal of fluid milk—milk destined for sale for direct consumption—was collected at farms and brought by rail to cities for sale and processing. As Chapter 5 explains, much of this early business went by express less-than-carload (LCL) traffic, with cans placed in baggage cars and billed individually. As railroads began hauling larger volumes and longer distances, railroads would devote entire baggage cars or specialized milk cars on busy routes.

For farmers who didn't deliver directly to creameries, this meant dropping off cans at the local railroad station or rural milk platform in the morning in advance of the train. Tickets were bought for cans (which were labeled), cans were loaded on railcars, taken to the city processing plant, and

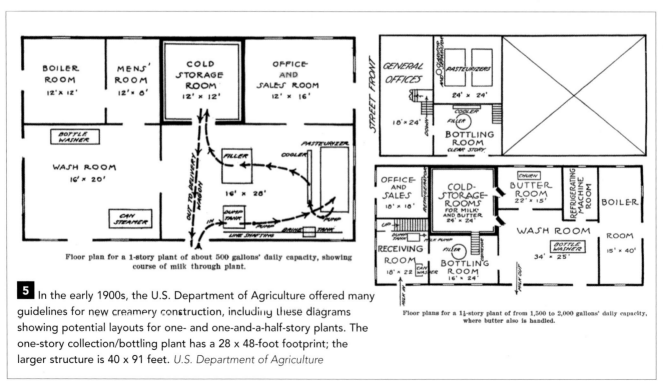

Floor plan for a 1-story plant of about 500 gallons' daily capacity, showing course of milk through plant.

Floor plans for a 1½-story plant of from 1,500 to 2,000 gallons' daily capacity, where butter also is handled.

5 In the early 1900s, the U.S. Department of Agriculture offered many guidelines for new creamery construction, including these diagrams showing potential layouts for one- and one-and-a-half-story plants. The one-story collection/bottling plant has a 28 x 48-foot footprint; the larger structure is 40 x 91 feet. *U.S. Department of Agriculture*

returned late in the day or overnight for the process to be repeated. This was a cumbersome process, tracking thousands of milk cans and getting each back to their proper owners.

The solution began appearing in the 1890s in the form of the milk collection station, **2**. These were also called creameries, collection creameries, receiving stations, country milk plants, or dairies. They were a key element of milk train operations in the Northeast and Midwest, found at almost every town (and often in rural areas) along milk-carrying railroads into the 1930s. Their basic task was to consolidate the output of several farms so that trains would make fewer stops.

These receiving stations were "creameries" in name only, as the basic ones did not do any processing. Farmers would bring their milk each morning, which included the previous evening's milking. The milk would be checked for quality, weighed, and transferred either to a holding tank or into one of the creamery's cans and placed in a cooling tank. The farmer's cans were then returned to him. Cans were kept in cooling tank and moved out to a trackside platform in advance of the next milk train.

Most basic facilities were small, one-story affairs, with wood construction. An attached icehouse (which was usually larger than the station itself) kept a supply of ice both for keeping the creamery's cooling tanks chilled as well as for purchase by farmers. In warm weather, farmers would often buy a block of ice to take home when returning in the morning. This was used to keep farm's cooling tank cool for the evening's milking.

Many collection stations were financed and built by railroads and some were independently owned. Most were eventually owned or controlled by larger dairy companies, **3**.

The coming of trucks and better roads allowed farmers to travel farther to bring milk to market, the result being that many small collection stations closed by the 1910s and later. The ones that remained grew larger and began producing butter, bottled milk, and other products. The trend

6 Can trucks, like this Bellows Falls, Vt., truck in 1939, handled milk can pickup and dropoff duties at most creameries by the 1930s. The milk in these cans would likely be bottled and on its way to Boston by rail within 24 hours. *Marion Post Wolcott, Library of Congress*

7 Many farmers relied on milk cans shipped via express in baggage cars. Here a cart of empties waits on a baggage cart at the Minot, N.D., depot in 1940. *John Vachon, Library of Congress*

continued toward larger and fewer creameries, with the Depression causing many marginal facilities to go out of business. Dairymen's League, for example, had 273 collection (country) creameries in 1930; by 1936 the number had dropped to 117.

Creamery design

A true creamery takes raw milk or cream and turns it into another product (usually butter), and may also process raw milk by pasteurizing and bottling.

Many combined processes: Producing butter, but shipping excess milk by rail or truck to larger centralizing creameries (more on those later), **4**.

Location was key, with the prime requirement being enough nearby cows to supply the milk and cream needed. Transportation for both incoming milk and outgoing products was vital. Many were built on rail lines, but this wasn't a requirement, especially for factories making butter or cheese. Most were built in towns or small cities, but some

Workers lift loaded milk cans to a conveyor at the Wilson Condensed Milk plant in Sheridan, Ind., in 1940. The cans are heading through the can door to the receiving room. *Linn H. Westcott*

Two route can trucks drop off their loads at the long conveyor at the Farmington, Minn., creamery in 1939. Each had picked up cans from multiple farms on their morning routes. *Arthur Rothstein, Library of Congress*

were in rural locations.

A good water source (well or city water) was vital, as even a small creamery (up to 1,000 gallons of milk per day) would use at least 5,000 gallons of water daily, and a large (5,000-gallon/day) plant could use more than 15,000 gallons of water daily.

That much water usage means a lot of wastewater output, which is why many older and small-town and rural creameries were located on rivers: They simply discharged wastewater directly into the river. In fact, early 1900s

USDA guidebooks on building and designing creameries referred simply to "drainage," pointing out that it was preferable to discharge wastewater into a running river or stream whenever possible "… so it is then sure to be no trouble from bad odors at or near the creamery."

This pollution issue was one of the reasons many smaller creameries closed from the 1950s and later, as laws began requiring treatment for sewage output.

Construction of many early creameries and collection stations

was often basic, and usually wood. By the 1920s, creameries were becoming larger and more substantial, and brick and concrete became popular as buildings got bigger and operations expanded. Wood construction had increased in cost, and offered no advantage: wood is not fireproof, and wood is harder to keep clean and sanitary. It's also more difficult to heat and cool wood buildings.

How a creamery is designed varies based on its size and what it produces. The USDA divided creameries into classes based on capacity and method of operation (see "Classes of milk plants" on page 31): Gravity plants were more expensive to build but considered ideal for sanitary reasons, as they avoided the use of pumps to direct milk around the plant. It can be labor intensive, however, to get cans to the upper level to start the process, and doesn't work with bulk deliveries, which must be pumped anyway. Few class 1 and 2 plants were built, and they tended to be large (like the big New York and Boston processing plants).

Class 3 plants were more common, where milk was pumped to a higher level (before being pasteurized), then traveled downward by gravity. Class 5 and 6 were the most common, and were largely smaller, older plants, often in rural areas—many handled less than 1,000 gallons per day.

In the early 1900s the USDA offered several basic design templates for creameries, 5, with suggestions on locating various features. Space is divided to keep related tasks nearby, and to keep piping runs to a minimum. Let's go through the basic features, facilities, and requirements of a typical creamery.

A boiler provides power as well as hot water and steam, needed for pasteurization and cleaning cans, bottles, tanks, piping, and equipment. The boiler room was usually located away from milk-handling rooms. Coal-powered boilers were common early, with a switch to fuel oil common by the 1930s and 1940s. These coal-fired boilers are the reason many early creameries had towering smokestacks, to lift the heavy coal smoke high and

Major dairy companies

By the 1940s, six major dairy companies dominated the U.S.market: National Dairy, Borden, Beatrice, Pet, Carnation, and Fairmont. Several other companies were major players in the major markets where railroads hauled milk.

In New York City, the Big Three were Sheffield Farms, Borden's, and United Dairy Products Co., which together had 60 percent of the market share. New York also had Dairymen's League (Dairylea), one of the country's largest cooperatives.

The major companies in Boston were H.P. Hood and Whiting; in Chicago, Bowman; and in Philadelphia, Supplee-Wills-Jones and Abbott's. The main producer of butter in the Midwest was Land O'Lakes (based in Minneapolis).

Abbotts—Large dairy company in Philadelphia. Closed in 1984.

Borden's—Gail Borden in 1857 formed the Gail Borden, Jr., and Co., starting by making condensed milk. The company grew to include bottled milk and milk products, and changed its name to Borden's Condensed Milk Co. in 1899 and simply Borden Co. in 1919. By the 1920s the company had 31 condenseries, two dried milk plants, two malted-milk plants, and several can factories. The company's Borden's Farm Products subsidiary operated more than 150 country bottling plants and 70 larger pasteurization plants. It is still a major national company.

Bowman—Started as a family business in the 1870s and known as Bowman & Co. by 1880. It became one of the largest dairy companies in Chicago, operating home-delivery routes and selling by retail. It also made and sold powdered milk and other products. The company was sold to Dean Foods in 1966.

Dairymen's League—This cooperative was founded in 1907 by a group of dairy farmers in Orange County, New York. It had grown to include more than 100,000 farms by the 1920s, and became the largest marketer of raw milk in the Northeast by 2001. It merged with Dairy Farmers of America in 2014.

H.P. Hood—Founded in 1846 in Charlestown, Mass., by Harvey Perley Hood. The company was the major milk supplier for the Boston area, and has since expanded to sell dairy products across the country.

Land O'Lakes—One of the country's largest cooperatives, it was founded as the Minnesota Cooperative Creameries Association in 1921 and became Land O'Lakes in 1924. Along with milk, it became one of the country's largest butter producers.

Sheffield Farms—The company was formed in 1902 as the Sheffield Farms-Slawson-Decker Co. with the merger of four large milk companies in the New York City area: Slawson Brothers, T.W. Decker & Sons, and two Sheffield Farms Companies (owned by L.B. Halsey and Horace S. Tuthill). By 1916 the company had 20 percent of the city's NYC dairy business. It became a subsidiary of National Dairy Products in 1925, but kept operating as its own entity through the 1950s. In 1925 Sheffield had 76 receiving stations and 13 bottling plants.

Supplee-Wills-Jones—Major dairy in the Philadelphia area, formed by merger of Supplee Dairy and Wills Dairy; was acquired by National Dairy Products in the 1950s.

Whiting—Originally D. Whiting & Sons, the company merged with Elm Farm Milk Co. and the C. Brigham Co. in 1922 to form Whiting Milk Co. It was a large dairy in the Boston area.

away from the area to limit chances of contamination. Large creameries might receive coal by rail, but local truck delivery was most likely for small plants.

Other mechanical equipment (pumps, refrigeration equipment) would usually be in a separate room as well. Mechanical refrigeration became common for creameries built in the 1910s and later, eliminating the large ice houses of earlier facilities.

Another important consideration was clean air: Creameries have a lot of vents and fans, with the goal to keep humid air flowing out of the building to prevent dampness and mold growth. Fresh intake air was often filtered.

Creamery processes

How milk got to creameries varied by size and location. For early small collection creameries, farmers typically delivered their own cans by wagon, pickup truck, or even automobile. Two

A milk tank truck drops off its load at the Enosburg Falls, Vt., creamery in 1941. Bulk handling from farms increased in popularity from the 1940s onward. *Arthur Rothstein, Library of Congress*

Two workers pour a can of milk into the dump tank in the receiving room of the San Angelo, Texas, creamery in 1939. Raw milk is sold by weight, not volume. *Russell Lee, Library of Congress*

or more neighboring farmers might share duties to conserve time and resources.

As farms and creameries increased in size and distances from farm to creamery increased, it became more common for creameries or private contractors to pick up milk each morning in can trucks, **6**. Large creameries might have a dozen or more trucks on routes to local farms, picking up cans in the morning and dropping them off later in the day. By the 1950s, bulk storage on farms and tank trucks for pickup became more common.

In areas where farmers relied on shipping cans to the nearest creamery by less-than-carload railroad express, a creamery truck would meet the train at the local station to pick up cans, **7**. Cans would be offloaded to baggage carts for transfer, and empties returned to carts for loading into later trains for the return trip.

Incoming milk cans enter the creamery at the receiving room, **8**, located adjacent to the truck driveway or delivery area. Typical operation was for cans to be placed on a conveyor outside, where they would roll either by gravity on rollers or by a chain

Milk cans are cleaned, sanitized, and steamed after each use, a cumbersome task. Most creameries had begun using automated machines for this by the 1920s. *Russell Lee, Library of Congress*

13 Milk is pasteurized before bottling. The creamery at Sheldon Springs, Vt., had multiple pasteurization tanks (each with a temperature recorder above it) in this 1941 view. *John Vachon, Library of Congress*

14 Milk is bottled the day it arrives, with the goal to bottle enough each day to fill the following morning's orders. This is San Angelo, Texas, in 1939. *Russell Lee, Library of Congress*

Cooperative vs. proprietary creameries

Creameries and dairies could be privately owned or cooperatives. Most privately owned (proprietary) creameries became owned or controlled by larger corporations (examples included Hood and Borden's). Small independents often made and marketed their own products on a local level, but often contracted with larger companies to produce their brands as well.

Proprietary creameries could include individual owners, partnerships, or stock companies. They purchased milk and cream from farmers at market price. Farmers could opt to bring their milk or cream to any proprietary creamery, but distance and the elimination of many smaller creameries into the 1900s often limited their options. Payment was made on delivery or at regular (weekly, biweekly, or monthly) periods.

As Chapter 1 mentioned, milk prices are volatile. Farmers had long been unhappy with prices being fixed by buyers, which by the late 1800s had evolved into several large dairy companies. Cooperatives were a way for farmers to have more input in the production and marketing decisions that affected pricing, with the farmers earning and dividing the profits instead of private companies.

In a co-op creamery, ownership was divided among member farmers who supplied it with milk and cream. They were run by an elected board of directors, which made decisions regarding production, prices, and marketing. Individual co-ops often joined with other co-ops to increase their marketing power.

Cooperative creameries became common in the early 1900s,

especially for those that primarily manufactured and marketed butter. Co-ops became most common in the Midwest: In 1921, there were 638 in Minnesota, 381 in Wisconsin, and 190 in Iowa, accounting for 75 percent of the U.S. total. There were just 26 co-op creameries in New York, 53 in Pennsylvania, and 6 in Massachusetts.

The largest of the cooperatives was Land O'Lakes, based in Minneapolis, with 320 member creameries in 1924. Dairymen's League was the largest cooperative in the East.

Cooperatives were not popular among private milk handlers, and private companies repeatedly challenged the legality of co-ops from the 1800s into the 1900s. Private corporations accused the co-ops of violating the price-fixing rules of the Sherman Act (of 1890), saying the co-ops were conspiring in restraint of trade (by collusion of individual farmers acting as a group to set prices), which was prohibited by the Act.

It wasn't until 1922 that the Capper-Volstead Act defined the legal status of cooperative marketing associations. The Act gave co-ops limited antitrust protection and gave farmers the right to act as a group.

Cooperatives usually did not purchase milk directly from member farmers. Instead the milk is processed, bottled (or turned into butter, cheese, or other products), and sold, with each member receiving a share of the profits based on the percentage of milk or butterfat delivered.

Many of these market their products locally and ship surplus to larger (mainly eastern) markets.

Butter is taken from churns and packed into tubs for storage and shipping. Wooden paddles are the standard method for handling butter. 1941. *Russell Lee, Library of Congress*

conveyor into a small can door into the building. This conveyor could be extensive at large plants, **9**.

For creameries using bulk trucks for pickup from farms, the truck tank will be connected via hose or pipe and the milk pumped to a storage tank, **10**. As more creameries began receiving milk in bulk, this was likely to be done indoors or in a sheltered area.

In the receiving room, each can is checked for quality, including bacteria and butterfat content (some creameries had a separate lab area). Once checked,

the milk goes to the dump tank, where it is weighed, **11**. The cans are then cleaned—this was automated at most creameries by the early 1900s, **12**. The cans are then routed out another can door and picked up by either the delivering farmer or stored for the can truck, which will deliver empties back to farms. (See "Milk cans" on page 33.)

What happens to the milk now depends upon each individual creamery. If it serves as a bottling plant, the first priority will be bottling enough milk to cover the following morning's deliveries

(including home-delivery routes as well as wholesale deliveries). The milk is pasteurized before bottling, **13**, usually in a separate room. It is then cooled and goes to the bottling machine, also in its own room to keep everything clean, **14**. Cases of bottles are put into cold storage until ready to be loaded onto wagons or trucks for delivery.

Bottling plants will have a washing room, usually adjacent to the bottling room, where incoming bottles are washed, sterilized, and stored.

Butter production is next (more on

Butter for consumer sale is cut and shaped by a butter printer, then wrapped and put in cartons and then cases. *Russell Lee, Library of Congress*

Butter has a long shelf life if kept cold. These wooden tubs are in a cold-storage warehouse in Jersey City, N.J., in 1939. *Arthur Rothstein, Library of Congress*

that in a bit). The churn or churns are generally in their own room, **15**. The butter is then either packed in large tubs for sale to wholesalers or brokers or it is packaged for retail sale, **16**. This is usually done in a packaging or preparation room, often called the "butter room." Butter is cut to shape by dies, either manually or with machines, called "printers." The tubs or cases are are moved into cold storage until ready for shipping, **17**.

Any daily milk remaining, and any milk that needs to be shipped to another creamery, is either loaded into a bulk tank railcar or truck or loaded into the creamery's cans, **18**, for loading into a rail can car or truck.

Individual creameries, of course, varied widely in layout, design, and size. Truck and rail docks and platforms would sometimes share space, or could be on opposite sides of the building. Creameries often had retail shops, selling milk, cream, butter, cheese, ice cream, and sometimes ice, eggs, and other products as well.

Centralizing creameries

Centralizing creameries are the larger operations in bigger cities that receive much of their incoming milk and cream from smaller collection or receiving stations in surrounding towns. They are generally the final destination for the milk coming in their doors, with finished products going out by truck or rail.

There's no real definition—most are USDA class 1, 2, 3, or 4 by the USDA. The large processing plants in metro New York and Boston are the largest examples, but almost every large city has one or two creameries that fit the classification.

For the "classic" milk era that we're looking at, a good example was the Sheffield Farms plant built in the Bronx in 1914. It was among the largest creameries ever built at the time and remained among the biggest for several decades, **19**. Located at 1075 Webster Ave., the building was 100 x 200 feet and five stories tall. It's believed to be the first class 1 gravity plant built, completely avoiding the use of pumps.

As with most large plants in the

A worker fills cans at the creamery in Burlington, Vt., in 1941. The cans will soon be loaded on a railroad can car and on their way to Boston. *John Vachon, Library of Congress*

The Sheffield Farms plant in the Bronx was one of the country's largest creameries when built in 1914. It operated into the 1960s. The archways at right were once open, covering the truck unloading and loading docks. This view is from 1991. *Historic American Engineering Record*

city, it wasn't located directly on a rail spur. All milk arrived by truck (cans into the 1930s, then transitioning to bulk), transferred from nearby rail yards. The archways in the photo were open into the 1950s, leading to the loading and unloading docks.

Incoming cans were unloaded, sampled, tested, and placed on a never-ending conveyor in a freight elevator to the fifth floor, where they were unloaded. From there the milk went to the milk room on the fourth floor.

Milk was initially processed through a clarifier (a centrifuge that removed dirt and debris), then passed downward through the pasteurization equipment. After pasteurization and cooling, it arrived at the bottling room

on the first floor. The milk was bottled and held in cold storage for delivery the next day.

The building had ice-making equipment on the third floor. Up to 50 tons were made each day, using brine tanks. The ice was crushed and traveled to the first floor in chutes and was used for cooling outbound loads in trucks.

Creameries like this were substantial multistory buildings featuring brick and/or concrete construction. The ground level would include loading platforms and often large doorways that allowed trucks to load and unload inside, **20**. Many of these had extensive fleets of delivery wagons, **21**, or trucks, both for home delivery and for sale to retailers and businesses.

20

Chestnut Farms Dairy, in Washington, D.C., displayed its fleet of delivery trucks in the early 1900s. The modern, three-story building featured brick construction and indoor loading bays for the trucks. *Library of Congress*

23

21

Horse-drawn wagons were the mainstay of home-delivery routes in 1910 when this view of the Detroit Creamery Co. was taken. The structure took up a large portion of a city block. *Library of Congress*

22

The Fairmont creamery in Crete, Neb., was a substantial operation, with a rail dock at left (and a North American Despatch reefer likely being loaded with butter) and truck dock at middle. The creamery also handled eggs and poultry. *Jeff Wilson collection*

Butter plants

Butter and cheese are produced by creameries and factories large and small. Butter and cheese making were centered in the Midwest, with much of the production shipped to eastern population centers (see "Butter and Cheese Production" on page 35). This was practical since both had shelf lives that allowed shipping long distances.

It takes about 2.5 gallons of milk to make 1 pound of butter (but this varies depending upon the butterfat content of the milk). This is why butterfat content is measured for inbound milk—the higher the fat content, the more butter that can be made with it. Creameries making butter receive either cream (that farmers have already separated) or whole milk. The cream is separated using centrifugal separators and the residual skim milk is set aside.

The cream is then pasteurized, cooled, and churned, which causes it to thicken, and the liquid (buttermilk) is removed. Salt is usually added—about 3 to 5 pounds of salt per 100 pounds of butter. The resulting butter is at least 80 percent fat.

Creameries producing butter generally store it on site in cold storage. Although butter has a

The Land O'Lakes creamery in Minneapolis, built in 1926 and shown here in 1929, stretched more than 500 feet with a continuous rail dock. It was one of the biggest butter-producing facilities in the country. *Minnesota State Historical Society*

relatively long shelf life compared to milk, creameries are limited by storage space, so they tend to ship it in large lots on a regular basis—often once or twice per week.

Into the 1910s, small creameries often shipped in less-than-carload lots to eastern brokers; these could be consolidated into full car shipments at intermediate stops (in the Midwest, at the Twin Cities or Chicago) bound for New York and other major markets.

Large creameries shipped out full carloads of butter, **22**. The creamery at Crete, Neb., also handled eggs, poultry, and milk. The huge Land O'Lakes processing plant at Minneapolis, Minn., could handle more than 10 cars on its building-length rail spur, **23**.

This butter was sold through several channels. It could be packaged for direct sale to consumers or to retailers, or sold either packaged or in tubs to jobbers and wholesalers, **24**. "Jobbers" function as distributors to retailers and other users such as restaurants and hotels, as well as buying products for resale. Wholesalers sell to a variety of sources, including jobbers, retailers, retail chains, and commercial users

(commercial bakeries, food processors, etc.).

The largest wholesale markets were Chicago, New York, Boston, and Philadelphia. Wholesalers often contracted on a yearly basis with individual creameries and cooperative associations, agreeing to take their output based on specific market prices.

The butter market tended to fluctuate, with late spring through summer considered a period of surplus production where wholesalers placed a lot of product into cold storage, **25**. By September 1, butter was being pulled out and sold.

Meanwhile, the skim milk left from the process could be sold as animal feed or used by food processors (candy and chocolate makers and others), delivered by bulk truck or railcar, **26**. It could also be dried and turned to powder for use in many products. This could be done at another facility, as we'll see in a bit.

Rail traffic for butter remained common through the 1940s. By the 1950s and later, refrigerated trucks were taking much of the business, although some is still shipped by rail, **27**.

Classes of milk plants, USDA

The USDA classified creameries (milk plants) by several types. As of 1920, they included:

1. Gravity, more than 1 story; Cans are elevated to higher level and dumped into storage tank
2. Gravity/pump, more than 1 story;
3. Pump to high level, then gravity;
4. Pump to high level, then gravity and pump;
5. Gravity, one story;
6. Pump, one story.

Largest plants: class 1 and 2 (at least 5,000 gallons/day); smallest, but most numerous, 5 and 6 (typically under 1,000 gallons per day)

Cheese factories

The first cheese factory in the U.S. opened in New York state in 1851. Cheese factories soon sprung up across many areas of the Northeast, and by 1900 Wisconsin and other neighboring states had hundreds of cheese plants. Much of the above description of butter plants applies to cheese factories as well. Most cheese plants are proprietary.

There are thousands of varieties of cheese, and the exact processes to make it vary by cheese type and size of the factory. It takes about 10 pounds of milk to make 1 pound of cheese.

To start the process, milk is brought up to the proper temperature (77 to 100 degrees), and a starter culture is added to curdle the milk. A coagulation product is then added, which causes the milk to begin to solidify. The solid is then worked to form curds, and then molded or formed. Most cheese is then salted and stored for aging. The liquid left from the process is called "whey," and can be marketed as a byproduct.

Few if any cheese plants received milk by rail. Some larger plants shipped by rail, 28, but it was more common for smaller plants to ship by truck or LCL, as the minimum for a full carload shipment (usually 20,000 pounds) was difficult for many small plants to achieve.

Condenseries and dried milk plants

Condensed and dried milk were developed to extend the shelf life for milk from days to years. They are also easier to store and ship than raw milk. The condenseries that produced these products were among the largest early milk plants, and they were served by railroads from the start, 29, 30.

Gail Borden was not the first to produce condensed milk, but he perfected the process and was the first to make it a successful commercial venture, and his company would become one of the largest dairy and food companies in the country.

Borden's breakthrough was in manufacturing method: The first step in making condensed milk is to boil it down to remove much of the water, but it was difficult to do so without scorching or souring the milk. Borden began experimenting in the 1850s, eventually adopting the vacuum pan process—since liquids boil at lower temperatures in a vacuum, the milk retained its taste and quality.

Borden opened the New York Condensed Milk Company plant in Brewster, N.Y., in 1864, which became successful largely from government contracts during the Civil War. The plant processed 20,000 gallons of milk daily. Returning soldiers contributed to the product's popularity, and Borden soon opened other plants (and

Butter could be shipped in large tubs or in retail cases. Here workers load a refrigerator car with cases of one-pound cartons of butter at the Land O'Lakes plant in Minneapolis in 1941. *John Vachon, Library of Congress*

Butter and cheese sold to wholesalers and brokers often wound up at cold-storage warehouses in large metro areas. This is the Seaboard Terminal and Refrigeration Company in Jersey City, N.J., in 1939. *Arthur Rothstein, Library of Congress*

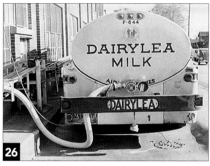

26

A Dairymen's League tank truck delivers skim milk to a chocolate factory in Syracuse, N.Y., in 1941. Bulk raw milk being transferred from railcars to city creameries would follow the same process. *John Collier, Library of Congress*

expanded to bottled milk and other products). Carnation, begun in 1899, was Borden's chief competitor for condensed milk.

To make condensed milk (also often called "sweetened condensed milk"), about 60 percent of the water content is removed in the vacuum pan process. Sugar is then added (about 40 percent), and the mixture is cooled and canned. The sugar acts as a preservative.

Production in the U.S. grew from 38 million pounds in 1890 to 186 million pounds by 1900 and 875 million pounds by 1917. World War I drove production even further upward.

Evaporated milk is made using the same basic process, but doesn't have sugar added. To make evaporated milk, after the product is canned the cans are heated under pressure to 240 degrees to sterilize the contents. The Helvetia Milk Condensing Company (renamed the Pet Milk Co. in 1922 after its main product) was the major producer.

In days before refrigeration was common, many families used evaporated milk to make reconstituted milk by adding water. Both products are also packaged and sold to consumers for using in food products (baked goods and as a coffee sweetener), and reconstituted evaporated milk was pushed as a safe alternative for infants and children where fresh milk wasn't available or wasn't of good quality.

Much of the sales of evaporated and condensed milk were to large-scale users, including companies making

Milk cans

Into the mid-1800s, the typical container for carrying milk was a wooden milk churn—the type used for making small batches of butter on a farm. As milk became a commodity, a better way of transporting it was needed. It was largely left to local tinsmiths to develop designs for durable, easier-to-clean metal containers. Soon many companies were producing milk cans commercially in large numbers (and in many sizes).

The 40-quart (10-gallon) milk can became the standard method of carrying raw milk from the turn of the century through the 1950s, and remained in use in many areas into the 1970s. Other sizes were also popular, namely an 8-gallon/32-quart version and a 5-gallon/20-quart can (popular for cream), but the larger can (or "jug") was most commonly found on railroad cars and trucks across the country.

Can designs varied slightly by manufacturer, namely in style and placement of handles and design of lids, but all 10-quart cans measured about 14" in diameter and stood 2 feet tall with a cylindrical body and angled shoulder with handles on each side. Most were stackable, with a lip around the base that fit over the top of another can. Through the 1940s, most cans were galvanized steel; stainless cans appeared after that, but rail use had dropped significantly by then.

Lids were either of two styles: flat ("umbrella") or with a depression in the top and a crosswise handle ("plug"). The lids simply pressed into place, which was a simple arrangement, but could cause problems. Lids would sometimes pop off in transit or when cans were handled or knocked together (or in extreme cases, if the milk or cream overheated and expanded), causing spillage and contaminated milk. Lids could also be difficult to remove. A mallet blow was usually sufficient, but workers would sometimes use any flat, solid object available to knock it loose.

An empty 10-gallon can weighs about 27 pounds and 10 gallons of milk weigh 86 pounds, so a loaded can was about 113 pounds—heavy but manageable. Creamery and railroad employees handled them with a mix of carrying and rolling (while keeping them vertical), and skilled workers could handle two of them at once with some leverage tricks. The cans' weight also made them dangerous, as a full can falling or landing on a foot or pinning a hand or arm could easily break bones and cause other damage.

One of the biggest challenges was keeping cans clean. After they were unloaded, they were given a cold rinse to remove any residue milk (hot water would bond the milk to the surface). They were then cleaned and scrubbed with soapy water, rinsed, given a spray of a cleaning solution designed to kill bacteria, and then given a steam spray as a final step. The continuous automatic can washer appeared in 1919, and most creameries soon installed automatic machines to take care of this process **12**.

The milk can is an icon of the dairy industry, but between labor, cleaning, and other challenges, it's easy to see why the trend from the 1930s onward was toward bulk storage and transport. Some farms and creameries continued using them into the 1970s.

Empty cans of various styles rest at the creamery at Caldwell, Idaho, in 1941. Cans were often marked with numbers or letters to indicate the owner. *Library of Congress*

Some butter is still being shipped by rail—in this case, at the Dairy Farmers of America creamery in Winthrop, Minn. The cars are Union Pacific mechanical reefers. *Jeff Wilson*

A truck is being loaded at the Kraft-Phenix cheese plant in Beaver Dam, Wis., which still had a rail spur in this 1940s photo. The plant was built in 1922 to make cream cheese. *Jeff Wilson collection*

Condenseries, which make evaporated or condensed milk, tend to be large buildings. The Helvetia (Pet) plant at Delta, Ohio, had a trio of Merchants Despatch refrigerator cars on its rail spur in the early 1900s. *Jeff Wilson collection*

baby formula, ice cream, baked goods, and other food products.

Dried (or powdered) milk is another way of preserving milk, and it's easier to store and ship than evaporated or condensed milk. Most common in early production was drying the skim milk left over from the buttermaking process (and dried whey from cheese), but there's also dried whole milk and buttermilk.

Drum drying was a common early production method, where milk is applied as a thin film to a heated rotating drum. The moisture flashes off and the dried milk is then scraped off the drum. This method could scorch

A semi unloads its cargo at the Wilson's Milk condensery at Sheridan, Ind., in the 1940s. The company made Wilson's Evaporated Milk, and also canned for other labels. It received coal and cans by rail and shipped out the final product by rail as well. *Linn H. Westcott*

The Land O'Lakes dried milk plant at Sebeka, Minn., had a rail spur on the Great Northern (note boxcar on left). Bulk milk trucks were unloaded under cover at right. *Jeff Wilson collection*

Cheese and butter production, Top 10 states, 1921

Butter production, 1921 in pounds

1.	Minnesota	149,522,200
2.	Wisconsin	124,987,100
3.	Iowa	106,118,300
4.	Ohio	78,691,300
5.	California	68,826,800
6.	Nebraska	66,663,500
7.	Michigan	51,700,200
8.	Illinois	48,135,800
9.	Indiana	46,493,900
10.	Kansas	42,415,972

Cheese production, 1921 in pounds

1.	Wisconsin	182,777,000
2.	New York	37,970,000
3.	Oregon	8,777,000
4.	California	5,904,000
5.	Minnesota	5,693,000
6.	Michigan	5,064,000
7.	Pennsylvania	3,208,000
8.	Idaho	2,117,000
9.	Vermont	1,380,000
10.	Utah	1,027,000

Production totals include creameries only, not farm-made

Powdered milk was stored and shipped in barrels or bags. This is at Caldwell, Idaho, in 1941. *Library of Congress*

the solids and affect the taste. A more common method became spray drying, where concentrated milk is atomized in a hot gas. The water flashes off quickly, leaving powdered residual solids.

As with plants making condensed milk, dried-milk plants tend to be larger than other creameries, **31**. They are called dehydration plants, dried-milk plants, or powdered-milk plants. They can receive milk from local farms; they can also receive bulk milk shipments by rail or truck from other creameries (skim milk from butter-making creameries, for example).

The finished product can be shipped to many final users. Dried milk, as with evaporated milk, was often reconstituted for drinking where fresh milk wasn't available, and it's used in many recipes, so it's packaged and sold for retail use. It's also used by food manufacturers (in candy, infant formula, and baked goods) and as a

component in animal feed. For this, dried milk would usually be packed in large barrels for shipment, **32**. Wood barrels were common into the 1940s, with cardboard drums after that.

Since condensed, evaporated, and dried milk don't require refrigeration, they could be shipped in standard boxcars. Refrigerator cars (without icing) were sometimes used for cased, canned food products because they were clean and offered protection from temperature extremes. Boxcars should be A or B grade cars, or those labeled for food products (plug-door and insulated boxcars became popular in the 1950s). Starting in the 1950s, powdered milk could be carried in bulk in the then-new pressure-differential covered hoppers, starting with the General American Airslide car (introduced in 1954).

Destinations for shipments include food wholesalers, grocery chain

warehouses, food processing plants, and government institutions. A good deal of these products were destined for export to many countries via ports on both coasts.

Some of this business still travels by rail, but most began moving by truck by the 1960s and 1970s. Also, the empty tin cans were often shipped by rail into the 1950s and 1960s. Barrels and other packing containers could also be shipped by rail.

1

CHAPTER THREE

Railroad-owned milk cars

A Central Vermont can car (No. 562), paint faded, is being loaded at the New England Dairies creamery in Enosburg Falls, Vt., in September 1941. It's one of 54 built in the mid-1920s. The standard Southern boxcar in the background likely delivered packaging materials. Jack Delano, *Library of Congress*

The first shipments of raw milk in the mid-1800s from country farmers to large cities were carried in churns, and most were carried in standard boxcars. This evolved to cans carried in baggage cars as express, and many railroads carrying high volumes of milk eventually built cars specifically to carry milk cans, **1**.

By the late 1800s, milk shipments—particularly in New England and the Northeast—were increasing by great numbers. Rail lines had expanded, track had improved, railcars were larger, and trains were faster than a couple of decades earlier. This enabled milk to make longer journeys, but with the increased volume, travel distance, and travel time, made it a challenge to get it safely to market.

The 40-quart (10-gallon) metal can had become the standard for milk transportation (see Chapter 2, Creameries and dairy processing plants) in most areas, and would remain so until bulk tank transportation became practical. These cans weighed about 27 pounds empty, and with a full load of milk topped 110 pounds—heavy, but light enough that a strong man could muscle and roll one into position by himself aboard a railcar, truck, or platform.

How to efficiently carry these cans was the challenge for railroads.

Baggage and refrigerator cars

In the early days of carrying milk, most traffic involved single cans or small lots of cans that traveled as less-than-carload (LCL) shipments. Because of milk's time-sensitive nature, shippers paid the premium for express service, which meant cans traveled in baggage cars on passenger trains, **2**, along with other packages, parcels, boxes, and crates. Some milk cans continued traveling this way through the end of milk service in the 1950s and '60s, especially for shorter runs on routes that didn't see a lot of milk traffic.

The main problem with this was to keep the milk cool in warm weather, especially when cans spent several hours on board. Blocks or chunks of ice were sometimes placed atop the cans inside the cars. This was reasonably effective at cooling the cans, but could make a mess of the car interiors and floors.

Another option was wrapping cans in blankets or canvas wraps, **3**. Although effective for short runs, this was impractical for large shipments of cans.

2 Empty milk and cream cans are loaded aboard a Denver & Rio Grande Western baggage car at Montrose, Colo., in 1940. Some milk cans continued traveling by baggage car through the end of rail milk service. Note the tags on the handles, and the beat-up state of some cans. *Russell Lee, Library of Congress*

3 Milk cans were sometimes wrapped to keep them cool, but it was mainly done by farmers in getting cans to the creamery or for small shipments in baggage cars. *Russell Lee, Library of Congress*

Also, on many routes, this extensive can traffic had greatly exceeded what could be carried as express or LCL in trains' existing baggage-express cars—a nice problem to have for revenue purposes, but one that presented challenges.

The emergence of the refrigerator car appeared to be a potential solution. The evolution of the ice-bunker refrigerator car in the late 1800s helped in handling many types of perishable traffic. The first true "reefers" appeared in the late 1860s, and featured an insulated body—usually double-sheathed, with both an exterior wood shell and interior walls, with some type of insulation between them. A bunker at each end of the car

This Wickes Patent refrigerator car was state-of-the-art when built in 1892. It's an all wood (truss-rod underframe) 32-foot car with ice bunkers at each end. It's not equipped for high-speed service, and rides on standard archbar trucks. Most reefers of the period were in meat or vegetable service. *Trains magazine collection*

Early milk cars often resembled baggage cars, as shown by Milwaukee Road 118 circa 1890. The car has a sliding door, clerestory roof, end platforms, and link-and-pin couplers. *Milwaukee Road*

Milwaukee Road No. 359 is basically an express reefer without ice bunkers. It has a wood body, steel underframe, high-speed trucks, and is labeled "EXPRESS & DAIRY." *W.C. Whittaker*

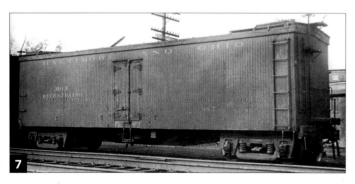

Baltimore & Ohio No. 847 is a former freight reefer the railroad converted to milk service in the early 1920s. *Bob's Photo*

held ice, with roof hatches above the bunkers to enable loading chunk or crushed ice.

Most early refrigerator cars were built for transporting meat, another highly perishable product, and by the 1880s refrigerator cars would be hauling a lot of fruits and vegetables as well. There were 1,310 reefers in service in 1880 (only 310 owned by railroads) but by 1890 reefer ownership grew to 23,570 (8,570 owned by railroads). In 1900 there were 68,500 refrigerator cars on the rails (14,500 owned by railroads), 4.

However, railroads have a long history of being reluctant to own specialized cars. There are two main reasons: they're more expensive to build and operate (requiring several thousand pounds of ice even for initial icing); and they will run loaded less often—half of their service time at best. This left private owners (shippers or car leasing companies, some of which were controlled by railroads) to build and own most of these cars.

For carrying milk, this meant that although reefers would seem to have been an ideal solution, railroads thought the expense was too great—especially since milk was a short-haul product (usually less than a day in transit) compared with most reefer loads, which traveled several days. The ice bunkers of a typical freight reefer limited internal floor space—limiting can capacity—and freight reefers were not equipped for high-speed service.

On the other hand, the growing milk business represented a lot of revenue—and potential revenue—to be had. The solution proved to be specialized cars, drawing on the designs and principles of refrigerator cars but with additional features to suit the product being carried.

Milk car basics

For a milk car—known also as "can cars," especially after tank cars began appearing—the basic requirements were capacity to hold a substantial number of cans, to keep milk cool for its journey, and to operate reliably as head-end traffic in high-speed passenger service.

Individual railroads and car builders approached milk car design in vastly different ways, resulting in a wide variety of styles of cars. Can cars tended to follow one of three basic styles: Some—especially early designs—looked like standard baggage cars, **5**, but with insulated bodies and floor racks or other designs that could handle water runoff from ice placed atop cans. Cars built through the 1890s and into the 1900s often had end platforms, end doors, and clerestory roofs.

Others looked like express refrigerator cars, typically with 50-foot nominal length, but lacking ice bunkers and roof hatches, **6**. The third variety looked like conventional freight refrigerator cars, but with high-speed trucks and passenger gear, and usually lacking bunkers and hatches, **7**.

Some railroads built milk cars new; others rebuilt old passenger or freight equipment for the purpose, usually baggage, express, or refrigerator cars, (and some railroads did both).

Let's start with the body. Most can cars were wood, since most were built in the 1920s and earlier, when wood construction was common for house cars. Cars were double-sheathed, with insulation between the interior and exterior walls. This was horsehair and other loose material on early cars, and cork and hair-felt blankets on later cars. The exterior sheathing was usually vertical tongue-and-groove boards. Although some cars were nominally 40 feet long, 50-foot cars were popular for the extra floor space and capacity.

A note on car length: Throughout this book there are references to cars being various lengths. When a reference is for a "40-foot car," this means nominal, not exact length. Car length is specified in many ways, including distance between coupler pulling faces, distance between buffers, or body exterior or internal length.

Roofs for the most part were wood. Round roofs were more common than peaked, with canvas/asphalt covering (most were built before steel roofs became common). Cars specified as passenger equipment did not require running boards, but some can cars

8.

Cans in this car are secured by wood planks placed in notches on the sides. Note the fold-down racks for a second layer of cans. Ice was chopped and shoveled directly on cans in warm weather. *Jack Delano, Library of Congress*

had them anyway (they were more common on reefer-style cars).

The majority of can cars did not have ice bunkers—it limited floor space and can capacity—although some did. Early baggage-style cars sometimes had two small bunkers on each end, with an end door separating them. More common practice was to place chunk ice directly atop the cans if needed, so floors needed to provide for drainage.

Doors, especially on early cars, were often sliding (baggage-car style) or inward-swinging (often paired). This was for clearance at many trackside platforms, which would interfere with outward-swinging doors. Many later cars had conventional swinging reefer doors.

Car interiors often had hinged fold-down racks, fastened to the side walls, making it easier to add a second layer of cans. Restraints were provided to hold cans in place so they wouldn't shift in transit. Wood beams or bars were typical, held by notches along the sides, **8**.

Like baggage and express cars, milk cars operated in passenger trains, usually as head-end cars (meaning they were placed between the locomotive

9.

Cars equipped for head-end service have a steam line (curved pipe under coupler), air and signal lines (right of coupler), and buffer (above coupler). This is a New York Central 50-foot milk car. *New York Central*

and passenger cars to make en route switching easier). This required them to have a steam line (used for train heat) along with a signal line and passenger-style brakes. Look at the ends of a head-end car and you'll see two hose connections (brake and signal) and a pipe for the steam line, **9**.

10

Starting in 1922 the Boston & Maine received the first of 25 new 50-foot cars from the Laconia Car Co. The cars were wood with two openings on each side, and had truss rods in spite of their steel underframes. *Laconia Car Co.*

11

Among the last can cars built were 35 all-steel cars for Boston & Maine. Number 1934 is one of 20 single-plug-door, 50-foot insulated cars delivered in 1957. *Scott A. Hartley*

12

Number 1909 is one of 15 mechanically refrigerated milk cars purchased by Boston & Maine in 1958. The 50-foot double-door car was designed to carry refrigerated cases of milk bottles. *Scott A. Hartley*

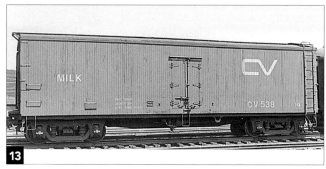

13

This view shows the final (1960s) scheme on Central Vermont's 40-foot milk cars, with the "wet noodle" logo. The fishbelly center sill is clearly visible. *Jim Shaughnessy*

That view also shows the end-of-car buffer above the coupler. Buffers were used on passenger equipment for absorbing impact forces during coupling as well as to limit slack action and other shocks when cars are in motion.

High-speed trucks were another requirement. Archbar designs were common through the turn of the century—and were even found on some new cars into the 1920s—but were banned from interchange service after 1938.

By the 1900s, drop-equalizer passenger-car style or other similar trucks were typical. A popular version was the Commonwealth from General Steel Castings. These had a longer wheelbase than the 5'-6" of standard freight car trucks: usually 6'-0", but up to 8'-0" for some longer cars, and often with 36" wheels instead of standard 33" freight wheels. Other less-common options were the Allied Full-Cushion, Chrysler, Symington-Gould, and Simplex. Some railroads reused trucks

from retired passenger and express cars on new or rebuilt milk cars.

The chart on page 47 shows Association of American Railroads (AAR) car classifications for various milk and baggage cars. As passenger-equipped cars, most milk can cars were designated BM: "B" for "baggage" and "M" for milk. Cars with ice bunkers were BMR ("R" for refrigerator). Some railroads listed their milk cars with their freight equipment, either as RB (bunkerless refrigerator) or XI (insulated boxcar), with a "milk" notation with the listing in the *Official Railway Equipment Register* (ORER).

By railroad

Because each railroad's cars varied, let's take a railroad-by-railroad look at key rosters. Only those railroads with significant numbers of cars are included. It's impossible to show all variations for all railroads, and photographic coverage for can cars was hit-and-miss, since most were built before rail photography grew popular.

The table on page 41 shows the number of milk cars operated by railroads for several years. These include cars listed as BM or BMR in the *Official Railway Equipment Register* or *The Official Register of Passenger Train Equipment*. It also includes cars called out as "Milk" in the *Register*, even if the classification is refrigerator car, insulated boxcar, or express refrigerator.

Excellent sources of information on these cars include the four-book series *Railway Milk Cars, Volumes 1–4*, published by Bob Liljestrand (Bob's Photos). The website of the New England, Berkshire & Western—the Rensselaer Polytechnic Institute's club model railroad—has a great deal of information on these cars as well at nebwrailroad.com. Individual railroad historical societies are another good source if you're modeling a specific railroad or era.

Baltimore & Ohio

Most B&O milk cars were older freight refrigerator cars that were converted for milk service starting in 1911. They retained ice bunkers and outside-swinging side doors, although a few were fitted with outside-mounted sliding doors. High-speed trucks, steam line, and signal lines were added. Early cars included class R-4 (Nos. 807-811, 813), and R-5 (800-804, 812, 814), all-wood truss-rod cars with archbar trucks. The "modern" milk cars were American Car & Foundry cars converted from 1921-1924: class R-7 and R-7A Nos. 824, 826-829, 834-837, 840-850, and 896-899, **7**. These had wood bodies but with steel underframes with fishbelly center sills and rode on cast-steel drop-equalized trucks.

Numbers 896-899 had pairs of 2,500-gallon glass-lined tanks—among the few railroad-owned tank cars. The tanks were removed in 1930-1931, but the cars remained in service another couple of years in can service.

The railroad also had four 60-foot baggage-style milk cars converted from former postal service cars: 820-823.

The railroad was removing milk cars from service by the early 1930s; all the older (R-4, R-5) cars were gone by 1935. Just 8 total cars remained in 1946 and the last cars were retired in 1951. The milk cars were painted coach green with passenger-style lettering.

Boston & Maine

The B&M had 37 milk cars on the roster by 1900, including some baggage-style cars with end platforms and sliding doors. The B&M's first major group of milk cars were 100 50-foot wood, truss-rod underframe cars, Nos. 1600-1699. There were 46 still on the roster in 1930; by 1943 they were grouped in the *Register* with other milk cars.

In 1922-1923 the B&M received 25 new cars from the Laconia Car Co. (in Laconia, N.H.), Nos. 1700-1724, **10**. The cars had wood bodies, no ice bunkers, with round wood (canvas-covered) roofs and two door openings, each with paired inward-swinging doors. Although equipped with steel underframes, they had truss rods as well. They rode on Commonwealth high-speed trucks with an 8-foot wheelbase.

In the early 1950s, 11 of these cars were rebuilt with mechanical refrigeration units and assigned as "bottle cars" (carrying bottled milk in cases) from Bellows Falls Creamery to First National Stores in Somerville, Mass. (the service is described in the operations chapter). These carried "Brookside Milk and Cream" heralds on the sides.

In 1953-1954, the B&M added to its milk roster by buying six of Erie's distinctive 40-foot steel reefer-style milk cars (see the Erie listing), numbering them 1875-1880.

Among the most notable can cars were the last ones built. Even though milk service was rapidly disappearing, the B&M ordered 35 new all-steel 50-foot cars from General American,

which were delivered in 1957 and 1958. There were two types: The first 20 (Nos. 1915-1934), delivered in December 1957, were insulated steel cars with a single plug door on each side, **11**. These were conventional can cars.

The second batch of 15 cars, delivered in January 1958 (Nos. 1900-1914), were mechanical refrigerator cars, **12**. They were insulated with two plug doors on each side and had the refrigeration unit mounted in the A end. These cars were designed to cover the Bellows Falls to First National bottled milk traffic, replacing the earlier wood cars.

These steel cars were all equipped with roller-bearing trucks (Chrysler

Milk can car rosters					
Railroad	**1920**	**1930**	**1943**	**1951**	**1962**
Arcade & Attica	—	8	—	—	—
Baltimore & Ohio	18	34	7	3	—
Bessemer & Lake Erie	7	8	—	—	—
Boston & Maine	92	71	57	49	35
Canadian National	—	21	14	13	7
Central Vermont	13	66	33	33	7
Chicago & Eastern Illinois	2	5	—	2	—
Chicago & North Western	238	254	102	39	2
Chicago, Burlington & Quincy	37	19	—	—	—
Delaware & Hudson	67	74	16	7	
Delaware, Lackawanna & Western	147	161	59	57	95*
Erie	66	346	135	100	95*
Grand Trunk	—	1	—	—	—
Illinois Central	1	2	—	20	—
Lehigh Valley	135	137	62	26	—
Maine Central	100	36	19	12	—
Maryland & Pennsylvania	—	2	—	—	—
Milwaukee Road	—	—	28	9	—
New York, New Haven & Hartford	126	100	35	—	—
New York Central	220	443	312	279	53
New York, Ontario & Western	113	253	14	7	—
Nickel Plate Road	—	5	—	—	—
Pennsylvania	38	113	—	—	—
Reading	27	27	9	7	—
Rutland	39	61	43	14	—
Soo Line	14	12	10	10	—
Southern (CNO&TP)	—	30	27	27	—
Wheeling & Lake Erie	4	2	12	—	—
* Erie-Lackawanna after 1960					

The North Western's 1911-built milk cars were 40 feet long with steel underframes and rode on passenger-style (7-foot wheelbase) trucks. The wood bodies had a centered sliding door. *Keith Kohlmann collection*

The majority of the C&NW's milk cars looked like standard wood reefers riding on high-speed trucks. Some, like 15298, had bunkers. It's shown in 1955 in express reefer service. *Keith Kohlmann collection*

trucks, which were comparatively rare) and were equipped for passenger service. The First National service ended after 1964 and can traffic had dropped dramatically. These cars were subsequently listed as freight cars, but most were simply stored.

Central Vermont

Through the late 1910s, the CV had but one dedicated milk car, with traffic handled in baggage cars or other (possibly foreign-line) cars. A series of boxcar-style cars were built in 1917-1918 (Nos. 501-513), with lengths from 36 to 40 feet. They had steel underframes and wood bodies. They were retired in the mid-1930s.

A new batch of 54 milk cars (Nos. 530-583) appeared in 1923-1926, built in the shops of CV and parent Grand Trunk. These 40-foot cars had steel underframes and double-sheathed wood bodies and canvas-covered wood roofs with a shallow curve, **13**. The cars had refrigerator-car-style outward-swinging doors with three hinges on each side; openings were 4 feet wide and 6'-3" tall. The side sheathing extended over the side sills by 5", leaving a noticeable step in the sill. They rode on Commonwealth-style high-speed trucks. The car interiors had hinged, fold-down decks to carry a second layer of cans; rub rails around the walls kept can handles from damaging the interior sheathing.

Starting in 1939, 29 of these cars were transferred to parent Canadian National; remaining cars were sometimes renumbered to fill gaps in roster left by the missing cars. A total of 26 remained in service on CV in the

early 1950s, but most were retired by the early 1960s.

As built, these cars had dark green paint with simple gold lettering. They were repainted in the early 1930s with aluminum sides with dark green lettering (with VERMONT MILK and GREEN MOUNTAIN ROUTE sublettering). This was again changed starting in 1938 to Pullman green with angled Central Vermont herald. These were originally separate metal placards but were later painted directly on the sides. The seven cars remaining in 1962 were reclassified as insulated boxcars and received the CV "wet noodle" logo and paint scheme.

Chicago & North Western

Early milk cars on the C&NW were baggage-style cars with single side doors. Early versions (Nos. 1410-1419, 1448, 1450) were all-wood with truss rods and end platforms. They were retired by the mid-1930s. Later cars (1452-1476), built in 1911 by American Car & Foundry, eliminated the end platforms, had steel underframes, and single sliding doors on each side, **14**. They were 40 feet long and more resembled refrigerator cars with high-speed trucks (riveted-frame with 7-foot wheelbase).

Next came the railroad's most modern milk cars, 100 cars built by Pullman (Nos. 15100-15298, even numbers only). Most were bunkerless, but the last in the series (Nos. 15260-15298) had bunkers and ice hatches, **15**. Another 100 nearly identical cars followed in 1923, Nos. 15300-15498 (even).

These looked like conventional freight reefers, with 40-foot wood

bodies and swinging reefer-style doors. The 1911-built cars had covered wood roofs, while the later cars had Murphy panel roofs. They rode on passenger-style drop-equalizer trucks (7-foot wheelbase) and had steam and signal lines and prominent buffers on each end above the couplers.

As the Chicago-area milk business moved to tank cars and trucks, most were removed from service (or reassigned as express reefers) through the 1940s and early 1950s, **16**. As of 1943, only the original 100 cars were still listed as milk (BMR) cars. The cars were painted green with yellow or white lettering, and "milk" lettering on one side of the door.

Delaware & Hudson

The D&H relied on baggage cars for most milk traffic until the turn of the century, having just two milk cars on its roster (Nos. 58, 59). A 1902 *Railway Age* article describes (and includes partial drawings for) what apparently are these cars, but doesn't identify them by number, just describes them as 52-foot truss-rod all-wood cars with end platforms.

The railroad expanded its fleet with 60 home-built 50-foot cars in 1907, eventually expanded to 67 cars numbered 800-866, **17**. These were 50-foot cars, all-wood with truss rods, but they were eventually rebuilt with steel center sills. The D&H started retiring them in the late 1930s, with 16 left in 1945 and 7 in 1949.

Delaware, Lackawanna & Western

By 1900 the Lackawanna had a substantial fleet of milk cars: 111

Several Chicago & North Western 40-foot milk cars undergo rebuilding in Chicago in December 1942 as some are converted to express service. *Jack Delano, Library of Congress*

mainly 42-foot cars (Nos. 1500-1610). These were all-wood construction with clerestory roofs and single doors centered on each side. They had ice bunkers and end doors (individual bunkers astride the end door). They were scrapped starting in the late 1910s.

In 1906-1907 the railroad acquired 25 longer (52-foot) cars (1700-1724). These were also all-wood construction, but rode on six-wheel trucks. They had arched roofs, ice bunkers, and end doors. They did not last long in service, and were off the roster by the mid-1920s.

The DL&W's first "modern" milk cars were 10 built in 1908 (Nos. 1611-1620), **18**, followed by 12 in 1911 (1621-1632) and another 10 cars (1633-1642). These were built by Keyser Valley Shops (New Jersey).

The original cars were 45 feet long with wood bodies, arched roofs, ice bunkers with roof hatches, no running boards, and a single centered door opening with a pair of wood doors that swung inward. The cars had end doors

with windows. They rode on iron-faced, wood-frame trucks.

The railroad bought another 110 cars, this time from Osgood Bradley, from 1924-1927 (Nos. 1643-1692, 1725-1784). These cars were nearly identical to the earlier cars, but with half-height (top only) end doors.

Many of these cars were rebuilt in early 1940s: end doors, bunkers, and ice hatches were removed; running boards were added, along with geared handbrake wheels and additional grab irons. Many were converted to express cars starting in the late 1930s, but a few of the later (1700-series) cars lasted until the Erie-Lackawanna merger.

The cars' paint scheme was Pullman green with simple Dulux gold lettering.

Erie

By 1900, the Erie had 43 milk cars on its roster (numbered between 1 and 99). In 1907 the railroad ordered 500 insulated boxcars from Berwick,

labeled as produce cars. They looked much like wood refrigerator cars, with reefer-style swinging doors, but without ice bunkers. They had steel underframes and archbar trucks and were not equipped for passenger service. However, several were rebuilt starting in 1923 with steam and signal lines, and a batch was renumbered 6000-6199 and classified as milk cars (BM). By 1931 the listing was 325 cars numbered between 6000-6549. Most were retired by the late 1930s.

In 1935 the Erie ordered the first steel milk can cars: a series of 55 40-foot cars from Greenville Steel Car (Nos. 6600-6654). Another 80 would follow in 1937 and later (Nos. 6655-6734), **19**. These were notable in that they were among the only steel-body milk can cars built, and they were delivered at a time when milk traffic was beginning to decline and remaining traffic was shifting to tank cars.

The Greenville cars looked like 40-foot steel refrigerator cars, but

17

Delaware & Hudson's No. 804 is a classic 50-foot milk car. Built in 1907, it has a curved roof, truss rods (later rebuilt with steel center sills), and inward-swinging doors. *Delaware & Hudson*

18

The inward-swinging doors are easy to see on Lackawanna 45-footer No. 1617. Cars in this series originally had ice bunkers like this one; many were later rebuilt and had them removed. *Bob's Photo*

19

Erie's 40-foot milk cars of 1935 and 1937 were the first all-steel milk can cars. They had Buckeye ends, Viking roofs, and trucks from older retired milk cars. *Greenville Steel Car*

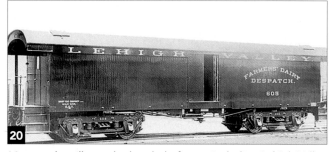

20

Many early milk cars had end platforms, including Lehigh Valley 605, shown around 1900. The car has inward-swinging doors. *Lehigh Valley; John Nehrich collection*

lacked end ice bunkers. They followed the basic construction guidelines for the 1932 ARA (American Railway Association) standard boxcar, and had 10-panel sides, riveted construction, and swinging side doors with an unusual-size opening (5'-6" wide and 6'-2½" tall). They had Viking roofs, a distinctive steel roof design with corrugations on each panel. Five of the cars (6666-6670) had racks for a second level of milk cans. All were insulated (AAR class BM).

The cars had distinctive Buckeye ends (with square corner posts), which the Erie also used on many boxcars. These ends have distinct horizontal corrugations (in a 3/3, or 3-over-3 pattern) that taper sharply at angles at each end. The cars also had geared vertical handbrake staffs—unusual for the period. As with other milk cars, they had steam and signal lines as well as high-speed trucks (6-foot wheelbase, drop-equalized) that the Erie re-used from its earlier converted refrigerator cars that had been retired.

In milk service, they were initially painted green with yellow lettering; then gray and green with yellow stripes and lettering.

By the 1950s, the cars were reassigned to express service (AAR class BX), and many had their swinging doors replaced by sliding baggage doors.

Lehigh Valley

Lehigh Valley's earliest milk cars were all-wood, truss-rod-underframe, baggage-style cars with end platforms, Nos. 601-670, **20**. They had single door openings on each side with paired inward-swinging doors. Another 50 cars, Nos. 671-720, are later listed as having steel underframes.

The LV modernized in 1924 by ordering 25 53-foot milk cars from American Car & Foundry, Nos. 1120-1144, **5-20**. These wood cars had steel fishbelly center sills, conventional outward-swinging reefer doors, and a curved wood (canvas-covered) roof. They had ice bunkers and roof hatches, but the bunker design was unusual in that the bottoms of the bunkers were elevated 27½" above the floor, allowing

one layer of cans to be placed under the bunkers. Interior length was 49'-4" inside at floor level, with 42'-7" between bunkers (for the second level of cans). Their listed capacity is 370 10-gallon cans. They were delivered with modified high-speed archbar trucks (36" wheels, 6'-1" wheelbase)—an unusual choice for the time they were built.

The railroad built 30 more similar cars in 1926-1927 (Nos. 1145-1174). In 1932, the LV built another nine (1175-1184); the main difference was using drop-equalizer passenger-type trucks.

The LV's milk car numbers dwindled in the 1950s; most were scrapped by the 1960s but a few remained in company ice service.

Maine Central

The Maine Central had several series of insulated boxcars (class XI) labeled as "Box, Dairy" in the ORER. Two series of these were also listed in the passenger register as well: Nos. 1506-1525 (36-foot, 70,000-pound capacity)

21

Maine Central's milk cars were classified as insulated boxcars, and were unusual in being single-sheathed with swinging doors. Number 1526 is a 40-foot, 40-ton car. *Standard Steel Car*

22

New York Central had the largest fleet of milk can cars, and most were of this easily recognizable design: 50-foot bodies with rounded roofs and deep fishbelly side sills. The paired doors swing inward. *Trains magazine collection*

23

Some NYC cars, including no. 6443, were fitted with early sliding plug doors. Some old lettering is showing through the new paint job above the "NEW YORK." *New York Central*

24

The New York, Ontario & Western had more than 100 of these 45-foot wood truss-rod cars in milk service. The squatty appearance and truss rods give them a unique look. *John Nehrich collection*

and 1526-1535 (40-foot, 80,000-pound capacity), **21**. These were the milk cars of the MEC.

Built in the early 1920s, they were unusual for insulated or refrigerated cars in that they were single-sheathed, with the steel truss body bracing exposed on the outside. This made them look like contemporary single-sheathed boxcars, but the MEC cars had outward-swinging refrigerator-car-style doors. The cars had steel underframes and wood ends, although a few were rebuilt with steel (Dreadnaught) ends and roofs in the 1950s. The cars rode on caboose-style trucks with leaf springs (instead of coil springs like a standard freight car truck). They carried MAINE CENTRAL and DAIRY PRODUCTS lettering.

New York Central

Early milk cars on the New York Central were built in multiple lots from 1889 to 1912 (Nos. 2071-2299) by Merchants Despatch (MDT) and the Central's own shops. They all followed the same basic design. They

were 50-foot all-wood cars with truss-rod underframes, single centered door openings with inward-swinging doors, and end doors. Similar cars were also built in 1912 and 1914 by MDT (Nos. 6200-6400).

Among the best known and easily recognizable (and the largest group of) milk cars were New York Central's 50-foot cars built by MDT starting in 1916 with Nos. 6401-6610, **22**. These were similar to the earlier all-wood cars, but had steel underframes with deep fishbelly-style side sills. This makes these cars easy to spot in trains. Bodies were wood, with vertical sheathing, an arched roof, and no bunkers, and ventilated openings were used on the sides and roofs. The cars rode on drop-equalizer trucks with 36" wheels and an 8-foot wheelbase.

Three styles of doors were used on the cars over the years: hinged paired (inward opening) with a rotating handle high on the right-side door as on the photo of 6535; an early sliding plug door, **23**, and a more conventional sliding wooden door with

interior tracks. MDT also built express refrigerators to the same basic design. Each car can hold 330 cans (single layer).

The 1930 ORER shows 334 milk cars in the 6200-6605 series and 59 cars numbered 8000-8059. By 1943 the listing had 57 cars numbered 5740-5799 and 255 numbered 6401-6660 (by 1951 the count was 56 and 223). Most were removed from service through the 1950s, and some were converted to baggage and express cars and renumbered in 1958.

Another batch of milk cars in the NYC family was a group of older 36- and 40-foot refrigerator cars operated by MDT subsidiary Eastern Refrigerator Despatch (ERDX reporting marks). As of 1930 this included 92 36-foot cars in the 800-999 series, a single 37-foot car (no. 1001), and 45 40-foot cars (Nos. 1002-1058). All had their bunkers removed and were classified RB (bunkerless refrigerator), but were labeled in the *Register* for milk service. They were off the *Register* by 1943.

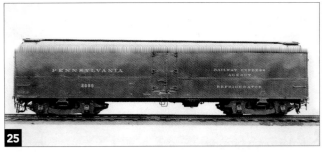

25

The Pennsylvania Railroad hauled most of its milk can traffic in its fleet of R50b express refrigerator cars. *Pennsylvania Railroad*

26

Rutland milk car 311 was built by Merchants Despatch to the same basic design as New York Central's truss-rod 50-foot cars. *John Nehrich collection*

New York, New Haven & Hartford

In 1930 the New Haven had 100 can cars listed (Nos. 24570-24791). By 1943 this had dropped to 35 cars (from 24720-24801), 40-footers with wood bodies and steel underframes.

New York, Ontario & Western

As a leading provider of milk into the New York metro area at the turn of the 20th century, the NYO&W had one of the largest early fleets of milk cars—113 by the late 1910s. Originally numbered 6001 to 6113, the earliest cars were built with end platforms. By the 1920s they had been rebuilt (and renumbered 1000-1113) to 45-foot cars with steel center sills (although they retained truss rods), and the end platforms were

27 The distinctive style of the Rutland/ New York Central milk can cars is readily apparent behind the locomotive (and to its right) on Rutland Train 88 at Burlington, Vt., in July 1948. *Jim Shaughnessy*

eliminated. Most were bunkerless, but some had a single bunker at one end. Single doorways on each side had pairs of inward-swinging doors. The round wood roofs were canvas covered and had running boards, **24.**

Many of these cars were equipped with Fox trucks—a distinctive early steel design—into the 1920s. They were then replaced with Wolfe trucks and trucks from earlier retired passenger cars.

In 1929-1930, the O&W reassigned 55 freight-service reefers to milk service and numbered them 1200-1254. These were 40-foot wood-body cars with steel underframes (fishbelly center sills) and archbar trucks, originally built in 1912. They were retired in the late 1930s.

The 1930 ORER listed 102 of the 1000-series cars and all 55 of the 1200-series cars still in service. The demise of can traffic and shift to bulk cars by many shippers on the O&W

led to a dramatic drop in car numbers, and just 14 of the 45-footers were left by 1943 and 7 by 1950.

Paint and lettering were simple, with Pullman green bodies and imitation gold lettering—railroad initials on one side, Milk on the other, with the car number under both.

Pennsylvania

The Pennsylvania Railroad carried a great deal of can traffic into the 1940s, and did it mainly in its fleet of express refrigerator cars, **25.** Express reefers that the PRR designated as milk cars in 1930 included Nos. 2500 (class R50 car), 2550 (R50a), 3026-3100 (R50b), and 5701-5736 (R60). All were 50-foot cars except for the 60-foot R60s. By the late 1930s, the Pennsy no longer designated specific cars for milk service.

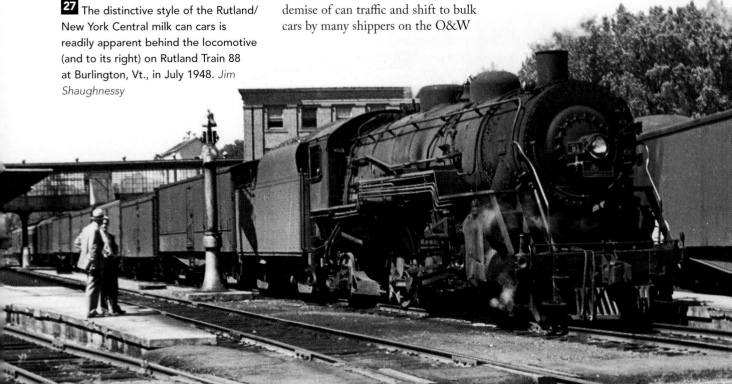

Reading

As of 1930, the Reading had 27 milk cars, Nos. 1567-1597. The cars were originally built from the late 1890s through 1923 and most were rebuilt or converted to milk service in the 1920s and renumbered to 1565-1601. The cars were a mix of either 51-foot cars or 40-foot cars converted from freight refrigerator cars.

Many were retired in the mid-1930s, with some lasting until 1953, as their need dropped with the switch to bulk cars by online customers.

Rutland

Rutland had several groups and styles of milk cars. The earliest cars were older baggage-style cars. They were originally numbered in the 140 series but renumbered into the 300 series in 1918 (numbers included 300 and 301, with 337 and 338 converted later).

Most of Rutland's milk cars were New York Central-style 50-foot cars, built by MDT. These were both the truss-rod-type with steel center sills (303-335), **26**, and the later style with fishbelly side sills (Nos. 340-349), **27**.

The railroad also had 14 milk cars converted from 40-foot conventional refrigerator cars (Nos. 388-399 in 1926-1927; Nos. 383-384 in 1948). These were steel-underframe wood cars with bunkers and hatches removed, but retaining their reefer doors (four hinges on each door).

In 1954 the Rutland acquired six former Delaware, Lackawanna & Western 42-foot milk cars (from the DL&W's 1924-built 1600-series). The Rutland repainted them and numbered them 350-355. These ran until 1961.

The Rutland had 61 milk cars in 1930, down to 43 in 1943, and only 14 in 1951 as most remaining milk traffic switched to tank cars and containers.

Soo Line

The Soo Line's first milk cars (originally Nos. 27-29; later 700-702, then 1400-1402) were built in the late 1800s. They looked like contemporary baggage cars: they were 52 feet long, had platform ends, single doors on each side, clerestory roofs, and all-wood construction. In the 1910s into the 1920s, the railroad converted 13 older wooden mail and express cars to milk service.

In 1924 the railroad built 10 40-foot milk cars at its Shoreham Shops. The cars (Nos. 2600-2609) look like refrigerator cars, and they were built with end ice bunkers (and roof hatches). They had steel underframes, wood-sheathed bodies with straight-channel side sills, fishbelly center sill, and a curved outside-metal roof. The top trim boards along the sides and ends give the cars a distinctive appearance. They had conventional paired refrigerator car doors, with just two hinges per door. They had Commonwealth high-speed trucks with a 6-8 wheelbase and 33" wheels, **28**.

The cars held two layers of cans, with a capacity of 475 ten-gallon cans. Hinged racks folded down from the sides and rested on the bottom layer of cans to support the top layer. They ran their last miles in the 1960s in LCL service.

Standard refrigerator cars

All of the above cars were used for transporting raw milk. For shipping finished dairy products—namely butter and cheese—standard freight refrigerator cars were the car of choice. Several photos of creameries in Chapter 2 show these cars being spotted and loaded.

Other products not requiring refrigeration, such as condensed and powdered milk, may travel in standard boxcars or in refrigerator cars without ice in the bunkers (which provided a controlled environment).

Most refrigerator cars through the 1900s were privately owned, as discussed earlier, with subsidiaries of railroads or car builders controlling the fleets. Examples include Fruit Growers Express, Merchants Despatch Transportation, Pacific Fruit Express, and Union Refrigerator Transit. Which company provided the cars to any given creamery or processing plant was a matter of what railroad line the plant was on, which refrigerator-car company provided "protective services" to that railroad, and whether the dairy company leased its own cars.

Milk car classes

Cars are classified by the Association of American Railroads (AAR) by basic car type and then sub-type. Although many are listed in *Official Railway Equipment Registers* (ORERs), many—as passenger equipment—were only listed in the *Official Register of Passenger Train Equipment* (ORPTE). Most milk cars were classified as baggage cars ("B"), with an "M" following to indicate milk service, as they were enclosed cars with high-speed trucks. A "T" suffix indicated an enclosed tank. The flatcars with milk containers were designated "BLF." Some milk cars with bunkers were classified as refrigerator cars ("R").

BM—Non-refrigerated car equipped for passenger service and used primarily for transporting milk in cans or bottles. Most railroad-owned milk cars were class BM.

BMR—Same as BM, but insulated with ice bunkers or ice boxes (similar to an express reefer).

BMT—Non-refrigerated house car equipped for passenger service, with one or more insulated tanks for shipping precooled milk. Almost all privately owned milk cars were of this type.

BE—Standard baggage-express car.

BR—Standard express refrigerator car; sometimes called out as "milk service" in equipment registers.

BLF—Flatcar equipped for passenger service to carry containers (specifically milk bulk containers).

XI—Insulated boxcar. Although technically not specified as a milk car or for passenger service, the designation was generally used for an insulated freight-service car; Maine Central, notably, had "dairy service" cars classed XI.

All above "B" cars must have steel framing, high-speed brake equipment, steam/signal lines, and high-speed trucks.

28 One of Soo Line's 40-foot home-built milk cars is tucked behind the locomotive as Train 2 rounds a curve near Duplainville, Wis., on its way to Chicago in 1949. *Jim Scribbins*

29

Land O'Lakes leased cars from Union Refrigerator Transit. Most were used for transporting butter from Midwest creameries to markets in the East. *Trains magazine collection*

From the turn of the 20th century into the 1930s, so-called "billboard reefers" were common. These cars featured large billboard-style lettering, logos, pictures, and other graphics featuring many companies' products, **29**. Although meat packing companies dominated, many dairy companies were included in these paint schemes, especially throughout the Midwest and plains states, which produced a large percentage of the country's butter.

The era of these colorful cars came to a halt in the early 1930s, when the use of billboard lettering was

banned in most cases by the Interstate Commerce Commission. The rule is complex, but the 1934 ruling was mainly about rebates from lessors to lessees. Railroads fought the actions of many leasing companies, namely the practice of lessors giving rebates based on cars' mileage income earned by the lessors. The ICC agreed with the railroads, and ruled that the large billboard schemes amounted to illegal rebates to the lessees.

Following the ruling—which took effect in 1937—a car leased by a single shipper (for example, a tank car leased to Sheffield Farms) could have that shipper's name and logo, but couldn't advertise specific products.

Decline in can car service

Although bulk milk cars began taking a larger share of the milk traffic from the 1930s onward, can traffic lingered for many years. Indeed, some creameries continued using cans into the 1970s, well after railroad milk traffic had ended completely.

Can traffic ended on some railroads sooner than others, and you'll find many cases of can cars from one railroad operating on another railroad.

The labor involved in handling cans was overcome by the development of bulk milk cars, which rapidly gained in popularity in the mid-1920s. The next chapter shows the cars that made it happen.

1

CHAPTER FOUR

Milk tank cars and containers

Workers transfer milk from a Borden "butter dish" tank car to a tank trailer in March 1940. The car, BFIX 508, is one of several that were rebuilt in the late 1930s. It still has its original separate letters applied to the hood. The scene is at New York Central's 130th Street Yard in New York, and the truck will soon haul the milk to Borden's plant at 110 Hudson Street. *New York Central*

Milk cans had long been used for transporting milk in all stages—from farm to wagon or truck to collection station to processing plant. Cans presented many challenges, however, and railroads and shippers had looked for viable options for bulk hauling for decades. The development of the milk tank car, **1**, dramatically changed how railroads carried milk.

The traditional 10-gallon milk can was versatile: It could be loaded in many types of railcars, trucks, and wagons. However, milk cans were labor-intensive to handle, had to be cleaned after each use, had to be kept cool in transit, were prone to damage from handling, and with tens of thousands in service, were a challenge to track and return to their proper owners.

Cans were also heavy—a 27-pound can held 86 pounds of milk—so a railroad car carrying 300 milk cans represented more than 4 tons of dead tare weight atop the car's own light weight to carry 3,000 gallons of milk.

Railroad tank cars had been around since the mid-1800s, and the first bulk milk rail transport was tried in 1903. However, the logistical issues of carrying bulk milk were more difficult than carrying kerosene, gasoline, vegetable oil, or other products that regularly traveled in standard tank cars.

The chief priority in hauling milk is keeping it cool during transport. This doesn't necessarily mean refrigeration, but it requires precooling and an insulated tank. Other criteria included developing a tank—in both design and material—that could be easily kept clean and sanitary. Securing the tank, having a tank durable enough to suffer the stresses of high-speed movement on track, and ease of loading and unloading were other factors, as was accomplishing all of this at a reasonable price.

Stainless steel—which would later be used widely for milk tanks and other similar vessels—was developed in the early 1910s, but its use was not yet widespread and its ideal composition (and methods for forming and joining) was still being developed.

The solution of the time was steel tanks lined with glass. The Pfaudler Company, led by Casper Pfaudler, had developed a method to line iron and then steel tanks with glass. Although an expensive process, the lining was strong, prevented interior corrosion, and was easier to clean as liquids were less-resistant to sticking to the glass than to other materials, including stainless steel. Pfaudler's tanks—as well as those of other companies using

2

This rendering shows how two Pfaudler tanks were placed inside a Baltimore & Ohio six-axle baggage-cars-turned-express-reefers in 1921. *Baltimore & Ohio*

3

The first production milk tank cars were three General American cars with Elyria glass-lined tanks. Each had twin 3,000-gallon tanks and ice bunkers. They were not equipped for passenger service. *General American*

similar processes—had found wide use in breweries and other food-handling factories, including dairies.

Early cars
The first known attempt to ship milk in bulk was in 1903, over the Boston & Maine from Bellows Falls, Vt., to Boston for the Boston Dairy Co. Few details are known, and it appears to have been a one-time experiment.

In 1910, two cars—each with a single glass-lined tank—were placed in service on the B&M for the same route (car nos. 12066, 12067), and in 1920 a car was operated by Whiting on the B&M from Johnsonville, N.Y., to Boston. These were precursors to later production cars.

In 1921, in coordination with the Baltimore & Ohio, Pfaudler provided 2,500-gallon tanks that were installed in three rebuilt B&O express reefers (two tanks per car), **2**. By insulating the tanks and installing the tanks

inside a house car—as opposed to in the open, as with a standard tank car—the temperature could be better controlled. The body would also protect all of the tank controls, valves, and fittings and provide a cleaner environment for the tanks. The cars were modified by removing the ice bunkers, reinforcing the frames, and adding tank cradles.

A test run from West Farmington, Ohio, to Pittsburgh showed the milk survived long trips with little change in temperature, and the cars and tanks proved to be easy to clean and efficient to operate. In August 1921, one of the cars was displayed at the National Dairy Show.

General American cars
Seeing commercial potential, car builder General American decided to offer a version of the car based on its 40-foot refrigerator car design, building them at its East Chicago

General American's upgraded design included a removable roof—note the lift rings on each side. The cars had high-speed trucks and passenger equipment, but still resembled refrigerator cars. *General American*

General American showed this cross-section view in its marketing materials to illustrate the car's features. *General American*

plant. The first customer for the car was Chicago's Wieland Dairy Co., which in June 1922 placed three cars in service carrying bulk milk from receiving plants in Wisconsin to its large processing plant in Chicago, **3**.

The cars were numbered 1X-3X (simply listed as 1-3 in the *Official Railway Equipment Register*) and received WDX reporting marks, but the cars were listed in the *Register* under General American. The tanks for these cars were built by Elyria Enameled Products Co., of Elyria, Ohio, and that company's logo was stenciled on the cars when built, with the line SEAMLESS ONE PIECE GLASS LINED TANKS. Pfaudler, which would supply all subsequent tanks to General American, acquired Elyria Enameled Products in June 1924.

On the outside, the Wieland cars looked like standard General American 40-foot freight-service refrigerator cars. They had insulated (Keystone hairfelt) double-sheathed wood bodies atop steel underframes with fishbelly center sills. They were equipped with

ice bunkers and rooftop hatches, and had standard swinging reefer doors with a 4-foot-wide opening. They were not equipped for passenger service: They had standard archbar trucks and lacked steam/signal lines.

Inside each car was a pair of 3,000-gallon tanks, cylindrical and positioned lengthwise in each end of the car. Steel cradles held the tanks, with the cradles attached directly to the underframe. The tanks were insulated. With its 6,000-gallon capacity, the car carried as much milk as 600 ten-gallon cans—equal to two can cars—a point not lost on shippers and railroads.

General American would go on to dominate the milk tank car market, although many upgrades and modifications to design would occur after the three first Wieland cars hit the rails.

Updated design

General American developed a new car design to make both construction easier (fitting the tanks) and making

high-speed passenger operation more practical. The bodies were still 40-foot and wood sheathed atop a steel underframe, but with no ice bunkers or roof hatches. Testing showed that the insulated tanks, enclosed in an insulated wood body, maintained temperature of precooled milk quite well (especially for the short-duration trips of most milk routes, where milk remained in the car for less than 24 hours). There was no need for the additional construction expense, loss of interior space, or expense of icing cars.

The updated roof was initially a patented single-piece removable design, **4**. This allowed easier, faster installation of the roof—it could be set in place once the tanks had been installed after the car itself was built. The thinking was that it also made it easier to access the tanks for repair or replacement later, a consideration that eventually proved to be unnecessary, and General American eventually changed to a conventional roof. Cars with removable roofs are easily identified by the four lift rings (two on each side) at the edge of the roof.

The new cars rode on high-speed trucks (passenger-car style with shorter wheelbase) and were equipped with a steam line, signal line, end-of-car buffers, and high-speed (passenger) brakes.

A distinctive feature on these and all future General American-Pfaudler cars was a small sliding access door just above the main side door or doors. This was used for connecting the loading hose while allowing the main door to remain closed, keeping the interior cleaner and minimizing contamination risks.

After the initial three Wieland cars, all subsequent General American cars used glass-lined tanks provided by Pfaudler. A tank was mounted in each end of the car, with an open space between the entry doorways, **5**. The tanks slanted slightly toward the middle of the car to make unloading more efficient.

At the end of each tank was a thermometer, a threaded unloading connection and valve at the base, and loading connections at the top, **6**. A manway with hinged cover allowed access to the tank for cleaning, required after every load was emptied. A blower supplying filtered air was provided in the carbody.

Tanks had internal two-speed agitators which stirred the load to keep the butterfat mixed with the milk (seen in the cutaway of the left-hand tank in the illustration). The motor for the agitators required external power and were only activated when a car arrived at its destination for unloading.

The tanks on some early cars were equipped with internal brine coils. These were used to cool the load, but were only connected while the car was at the loading creamery. They were found to be unnecessary, provided that the milk had already been precooled to the desired temperature.

Milk was unloaded either via a pump or compressed air. The compressed air system was more common, probably for the ease of cleaning compared to a pump.

Cars also included electric lights. There was no on board electrical supply for the lights, pump, agitator, or other accessories—a power cord would be plugged in while the car was parked.

To demonstrate how well the cars performed, a test trip was made in February 1925 with a load of milk from Marshfield, Wis., to Miami, Fla. During the 101-hour trip, the temperature of the milk was less than 2 degrees warmer than when loaded.

The next major design revision was 50-foot cars, **7**. The design remained similar, but the increased length made them look more like an express reefer without ice hatches. The cars still had swinging-type doors, but with a 5-foot opening instead of the 4-foot opening of the 40-footers. The cars no longer used removable roofs, instead using rounded roofs.

These cars quickly became popular among dairy companies, and by 1930, about 300 were in service. By 1932, tank cars were carrying 44 percent of Boston's inbound milk; the following year it was more than half, at 60 percent.

Early General American-Pfaudler cars were bought or leased by Borden's,

6 A bit of milk spilled from the bottom tank outlet inside a GPEX car, which has just begun transloading to a truck. Note the manway and thermometer (to the worker's left) and the power cord. *Arthur Rothstein, Library of Congress*

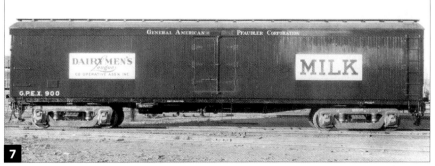

7 The first 50-foot wood cars, like this one leased to Dairymen's League, had 5-foot door openings, rounded roofs, and Commonwealth-style trucks. *General American*

53

8 Built in 1927, wood car No. 779 still wears the original GARE reporting marks and pre-GPEX General American Refrigerator Express lettering. *General American*

9 Sheffield Farms owned this 40-foot General American car, built in 1928. Large signboards were common through the 1930s on milk tank cars. *General American*

10 Dairymen's League leased this 1927-built 50-foot car. It features painted lettering instead of signboards, and shows how multiple lettering and paint schemes were provided for lessees. *General American*

Capitol Dairy (Chicago), Dairymen's League (New York), Sheffield (Sealtest), Abbotts (Philadelphia and Atlantic City), Seminole Milk Co. (Jacksonville, Fla.), Producers Milk Co. (Waterloo, Iowa), and many others.

Most cars leased by GA initially had GARE reporting marks, usually with "General American Refrigerator Express" lettering above the door, **8**. This grouped the milk cars with the rest of the company's general refrigerator-car fleet. As of 1930, there were 100 cars in the fleet, nos. 700-799.

In 1930 General American and Pfaudler formed a new subsidiary company, General American-Pfaudler Corporation, to manage these of cars. Reporting marks were changed to GPEX and the above-door lettering to "General American-Pfaudler Corporation." Earlier cars were subsequently relettered.

Other lettering on cars varied quite

a bit into the 1930s. Many of the wood cars carried large lettering and logos or heralds for their owners or lessees, often on separate panels attached to the car sides, **9, 10**.

Steel cars

A chronic problem with wood refrigerator cars was that the vertical tongue-and-groove side sheathing needed frequent repainting and repair, and often replacement—water seeping in would damage the insulation and the wood siding itself. General American began building new steel cars and rebuilding many older cars with steel sides beginning around 1935, **11**.

These cars were distinctive, standing out prominently in photos of milk trains from this period onward. The sides were vertical sheets with riveted joints, and the steel roof wrapped around over the side panels in a tight radius. The cars had a single narrow (2'-6") door opening on each side, and most cars had a single door but some early cars had a pair of narrow doors, **12**. Since bulk cars only required worker access and didn't require the space to move cases, cans, or crates, narrowing the opening (the doors were closed whenever possible) reduced the risk of contamination of the inside of the car, which was kept as clean as possible.

The ends were smooth, with three vertical steel riveted panels. Grab irons were used instead of ladders on both ends and sides. The smooth sides meant the coupler and buffer stood out on the ends. The B (brake) ends had a high-mounted brake wheel, retainer valve, and brake platform.

Rebuilt cars can be spotted by their straight sides along the bottom sill (with exposed channel) and their fishbelly style center sill, as on No. 544. New steel cars had sides that curved at the bottom, wrapping around the side sill, and had straight underframes (no visible center sill), **13**. Many new cars also had Symington high-speed trucks instead of the passenger-style trucks of older cars, as on No. 916.

The 40-foot length remained most common for GPEX cars through the steel car era. Most 50-foot steel cars had pairs of 4,000-gallon tanks for an 8,000-gallon capacity, but some remained at 6,000 gallons—see the chart on page 64. The last batches of these cars were built in 1947.

The standard paint scheme for steel cars was a dark olive green with gold or white lettering. Lettering was simplified compared to the wood cars (see the restrictions on billboard lettering for reefers in Chapter 3), **14**. Some early cars had large sign boards, but by the end of World War II, most wore basic lettering: to the left of the door was lettered the owning or leasing company (this was painted on some cars) in Roman lettering, with "LESSEE" in smaller lettering underneath it, plus the reporting marks and number. To the right of the door was "MILK TANK CAR" or "MILK REFRIGERATOR."

Merchants Despatch

Although General American built the majority of milk tank cars, a significant number of cars was also built by Merchants Despatch Transportation (MDT). Merchants Despatch was a car-building subsidiary of the New York Central that also operated and leased refrigerator cars and provided protective service (icing).

The company had built many refrigerator cars and milk can cars, notably NYC's distinctive 50-footers. MDT built five lots of 20 tank cars from 1926 through 1930 (each lot was divided among multiple buyers) for Borden's, Bowman, Hood, and Supplee-Jones-Wills. All were 40-foot cars with twin 3,000-gallon Pfaudler tanks. No cars were built after 1930, likely because Pfaudler became an official partner with General American.

Early MDT tank cars looked like a contemporary MDT refrigerator car. The first (Bowman 101-series in 1926) had a wood body and peaked roof, with the MDT-style fishbelly center sill and straight side frames. They had standard swinging refrigerator doors with a small access opening and plug above the door (similar to the GA cars). They rode on high-speed trucks and had passenger gear (steam and signal lines, buffers).

MDT then built several cars for Borden's Farm Products (Chicago,

Private-owner milk tank cars

Railroad	Rep. Marks	1930	1943	1951	1962
Abbotts Dairies	ADX	—	11	4	—
Borden's Farms	BFIX	35	43	41	—
Borden-Wieland (Chic.)	BWIX	26	5	—	—
Borden Mfd. Prod. Div.		—	—	3	—
Bowman Dairy	BOWX	40	31	29	—
Cloverland Dairy	CDPX, BCRX	—	4	—	—
Commodities Car Co.	CMWX	—	5	20	25
Co-op Dairies		18	—	—	—
* Gen. American-Pfaudler	GARE, GPEX	100	208	292	151
Merchants Despatch	MDT	87	57		—
** National Car Co.	NX	—	32	101	23
North American		1	—	—	—
*** Pioneer Ice Cream		—	—	2	—
Sheffield Farms	SFCX	57	59	5	—
Supplee-Wells-Jones	SWJX	21	20	9	—
Whiting Milk Co.		—	—	4	

* Originally GARE, then GPEX after 1930. Cars were leased to a number of dairy companies (including many who also owned their own cars as well).

** Flatcars for carrying tank containers.

*** Division of Borden

Sources: *Official Railway Equipment Register, Official Register of Passenger Train Equipment*, various issues

Ownership and leasing

The development of bulk milk cars led to a change in ownership. Whereas railroads owned almost all of the can cars, private owners (dairy companies or car leasing companies) would own all bulk cars except for the early experimental B&O cars. The trend followed that of other specialized equipment, namely general-service tank cars and ice-bunker refrigerators.

Railroads, always reluctant to invest in specialty cars, were happy to leave ownership to others. The new bulk milk cars represented a significant investment in equipment, and unlike can cars, they weren't suitable for conversion to express, baggage, or refrigerator service. The chart above shows ownership of tank cars across several years.

Some dairy companies purchased cars outright; most leased their cars from General American-Pfaudler (even those that owned cars usually leased additional cars). The usual lease agreement was

General American-Pfaudler operated the largest fleet of milk tank cars. Number 994, a 40-foot steel car, was leased to H.P. Hood & Sons at the time of this 1963 photo. *Jim Shaughnessy*

generally 5 or 7½ years. Lessees paid a per diem (daily) rate ($7 in the late 1920s for a 6,000-gallon cars). Railroads in turn paid a mileage fee to the lessor (2 cents per mile at that time), which was credited to the lessee's account. The result was an incentive to keep cars moving and working.

Number 544 was rebuilt from an earlier 40-foot wood car in 1938. Note the straight bottom of the side where it meets the channel side sill. Roofs wrapped around to the sides in a tight curve. *General American*

Number 766 is a 40-foot steel car rebuilt from a wood car. It has a narrow (2'-6") door opening with a pair of doors. Signboards proclaim that it is leased to Sheffield Farms. *General American*

Steel 40-footer No. 916 was built new, identifiable by the curved bottom side and lack of a fishbelly center sill. It rides on Symington trucks and has the standard narrow door opening but paired narrow doors. *General American*

BFPX) with clerestory roofs—very unusual for the period. The final MDT design had a rounded roof with prominent channel side sills, **15**.

Borden "butter dish" and similar cars

In 1936, Borden's company shops began rebuilding many of its older MDT wood-body tank cars, **16**, which were originally built starting in 1926, and the result was 35 unique bulk milk cars. They retained the two 3,000-gallon tanks of the earlier wood cars, but with a streamlined hood-style superstructure that covered the tanks, **1, 17**.

These cars have been nicknamed "butter dish" cars for their appearance, and also have provoked comments that they look like an inverted bathtub on a flatcar. Their distinctive style has made them favorites of modelers and railfans alike, with an interest level quite high considering how comparatively few were actually built.

Borden removed the car superstructure but left the car's frame with its distinctive channel side sills. The tanks were insulated with 6" of cork, with another 6" inside the hood. The hood, contoured with sloping ends, a curved top, and vertical sides, was formed from sheet steel with aluminum fused to the exterior surface. As built the cars had decorative aluminum fins centered along the length of the car and following down each end. These were short-lived, as the top fins were removed as a contribution to a World War II scrap drive in the early 1940s (they remained on the car ends).

The hood was secured in place on the frame—it was not designed to be easily removable. A door on each side allowed access to tank controls and plumbing, much like the enclosed refrigerator-car-style cars.

Along with the advantage of swapping the maintenance-heavy wood superstructure for steel, another benefit of the Borden rebuild was the weight—the hood was much lighter compared to the body structure of a house car. The light weight of a rebuilt Borden car was 84,000 pounds, three tons lighter than the 90,000 pounds of the original MDT car. A Borden's ad of the period touted that the empty car weighed 42 tons and a loaded car 67 tons.

A news release in February 1936 called the car "the first all-metal, stream-line milk tank railroad car ever built." There has been some confusion over the cars' capacities over the years, no doubt dating back to the original news release which states the car has "two 12,000-quart" tanks. Some sources have incorrectly listed each car's capacity as 12,000 gallons (including editions of the *Car Builders' Cyclopedia*)—the car capacity was 6,000 gallons.

The cars had BFIX reporting marks and were numbered in the 500 series, but Borden didn't track which cars were rebuilt (and many photos show butter-dish cars in operation next to unrebuilt wood cars from the same series). Known rebuilds include 503, 516, 520-523, 527, 531, and 534.

The cars were originally painted white or aluminum and lettered with individual yellow sheet-metal letters bolted to the hood. By the late 1940s the bodies were painted red-orange with yellow lettering. The cars' final scheme, by the 1950s, was aluminum with black lettering.

As milk service dropped off, many of the hooded cars finished their careers with Borden's chemical and glue divisions. Cars reassigned to this service received BCDX reporting marks and were renumbered to the 1000 series.

General American-Pfaudler also rebuilt four similar cars in 1940 (Nos. 801-804), **18**, from earlier wood cars. They are distinctively different compared to Borden's cars, with a taller hood profile that doesn't slope as steeply at the ends compared to the Borden cars. They also lack the decorative fins and have different frames and placement of brake wheels.

Their side details are similar to the GA-Pfaudler steel house cars, with a narrow access door on each side, and a small sliding access door above it. The side handrails continue straight across the side doors. Their capacity was also unusual, with two

Milk tank car classes

Cars are classified by the Association of American Railroads (AAR) by basic car type and then sub-type (designations were originally assigned by the Master Car Builders, MCB). Although many are listed in the *Official Railway Equipment Registers* (ORER), many—as passenger equipment—were only listed in the *Official Register of Passenger Train Equipment* (ORPTE), which began as a separate publication in 1943.

Most milk cars were classified as baggage cars ("B"), with an "M" following to indicate milk service; a "T" suffix indicated an enclosed tank (thus most of these cars were "BMT." The flatcars with milk containers were designated "BLF."

BMT—Non-refrigerated house car equipped with one or more insulated tanks for shipping precooled milk. Most privately owned milk cars were of this type.

BE—Standard baggage-express car.

BR—Standard express refrigerator car.

BLF—Flatcar equipped for passenger service to carry containers (milk bulk containers).

All above cars must have steel framing, high-speed brake equipment, steam/signal lines, and high-speed trucks.

The 50-foot steel version was the final development of General American-Pfaudler cars. Number 1025, built in 1947 and leased to Chicago's Bowman Dairy, has a pair of 4,000-gallon tanks. *General American*

Supplee No. 6, a late MDT car built in 1930, has the distinctive separate letters that make the brand's cars stand out. MDT cars lacked the trim boards of the General American wood cars. It's being switched on the Huntington & Broad Top. *Al Rung*

One of Borden's wood-body MDT-built tank cars is tucked behind Rutland 4-6-0 No. 45. Borden began rebuilding these cars into streamlined ("butter dish") cars beginning in 1936. *Trains magazine collection*

3,800-gallon tanks for a total capacity of 7,600 gallons.

Loading and unloading

Once an empty car was set out at a creamery, it would be "blue-flagged"— blue tags placed on each end of the car to alert railroad crews not to move or couple to the car, as workers were on it. These flags could only be removed by the workers who placed them.

Creamery employees connected piping from the building's storage tank to the tank car. The side door on the car would be opened, but the small access door above the main door was used for the piping whenever possible. Threaded couplings were used for connections— note the worker with a wrench in **19**.

When loading was finished, the piping was disconnected, doors sealed, and blue flags removed. Creameries would time loading so that the car would not sit long before being picked up by a train. Some early cars were equipped with internal brine coils, so the creamery would connect a line to this connection and pump a sub-freezing brine mixture through the coils until the car was picked up.

Upon arrival at its destination, it was set out and again blue-flagged, **20**. This could be at a siding at the receiving plant, or at a yard or team track (the most likely scenario in Boston and New York), with a tank truck parking next to it to make the transfer.

A power cable would be connected to the car and the internal agitators turned on. This mixed the cream back into the milk (it tended to separate and float on top), helping it drain better. A flexible hose with threaded coupling was connected to the lower outlet valve on a tank with the other end to the stationary tank at the receiving plant or to the inlet of a tank truck, **21**. The car's compressor or pump would be turned on to empty the tank, with the process repeated for the second tank.

Once the car was empty it was cleaned. This required a worker to open the manway at the end of the tank inside the car, then rinse, sterilize, and steam the tank. The car would then be ready to head back for its next load.

Milk containers

With the proliferation of today's container traffic and solid trains of

double-stack well cars, it can be hard to remember that the milk industry in the 1930s was a pioneer in intermodal traffic, with tank containers that could be transferred from flatcars to truck chassis as needed, **22**.

The idea of containers for less-than-carload (LCL) freight had actually been put into service earlier, with the New York Central and Pennsylvania Railroad both acquiring significant equipment by 1920.

A Lexington, Ky., entrepreneur named Benjamin Franklin Fitch had in 1917 developed plans for containers that could be easily transferred from flatcars to trucks to storage areas, mainly for carrying LCL. Fitch partnered with truck builder White to start the Motor Terminals Company (later Motor Terminals Inc., or MTI).

By the 1920s, the Pennsylvania Railroad and New York Central were both using containers for LCL on several routes, from small 8-foot-square boxes to large 20-foot boxes that required a trailer chassis.

A variety of factors in the 1920s and '30s, including federal rate restrictions, limited more widespread use of LCL containers, so Fitch looked for new markets. He saw potential in milk transport in the Northeast.

Milk tank cars were already gaining in popularity, with many shippers leasing or buying their own. However, although milk tank cars streamlined operation and had many advantages over the inefficiencies of cans, they still required that milk be transferred to tank trucks for the final movement to city processing plants. This required time for the transfer, not to mention the investment in the tank truck equipment.

Fitch's idea was to use tank containers that could be easily moved between flatcars and truck chassis. His initial thought was that tank containers could be all-purpose—four-purpose according to the original marketing materials: storage in collection creameries; transport on railcar; transport on truck; and storage at the final processing/bottling plant.

Fitch envisioned his system replacing storage tanks at collection creameries, or even allowing farmers to fill tanks and bypass collection

This heavily retouched publicity photo shows one of Borden's streamlined cars as built, with the decorative fin along the top and ends. *Borden*

creameries entirely, with trucks carrying tanks to a railroad connection. The idea of bypassing the collection station didn't pan out, but his system and ideas had enough merit that railroads and dairy companies showed interest.

Initial tanks on O&W

In 1935 the New York, Ontario & Western began working with Motor Terminals Inc., to put Fitch's ideas into action. The railroad modified a pair of

flatcars (nos. 3029, 3034) to each hold four 2,000-gallon (later 2,500-gallon) tanks. The tanks, which looked like those mounted on straight-frame truck chassis but with flat bottoms, were designed to mount transversely on the flatcar, **23**.

The tank containers were 8 feet long with the tank itself having a horizontal-oval cross section. The internal tank was stainless steel, with 2½ inches of insulation separating it from an outer welded steel shell. Tanks

General American rebuilt four older cars with hoods, including No. 803 (at left). It and 50-foot wood car GPEX 975 are leased to H.P. Hood and being switched on the St. Johnsbury & Lamoille County at Cambridge Junction, Vt., in 1946. *Philip R. Hastings*

19 A worker tightens a connection to ready a Borden car for loading at a collection creamery in 1947. Note the heavy insulation on the door, and that the car still has the separate metal letters applied to the hood. Precise spotting of the car is required for alignment of the loading pipe. Both photos: *New York Central*

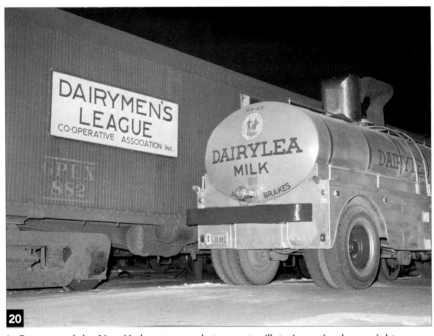

20 In Boston and the New York metro markets, most milk trains arrived overnight. Power cables have been connected to the car (they're visible under the carbody). This is Jersey City, N.J., in April 1939. *Arthur Rothstein, Library of Congress*

were loaded via a top-center hatch and unloaded by a lower pipe and valve. Structural steel cradles under the tank were covered by sheet-metal skirting. Under the base were a pair of runners to match skid rails on the flatcar and truck chassis for alignment.

To convert a flatcar to tank container service, the car received reinforced side frames (to support the weight of the tank during transfer), skid rails on the deck to align and guide the tanks, anchors at each end of the tank locations, and collapsible hinges along the sides to provide a physical connection to the highway truck chassis.

The flatcars were equipped for passenger-train service. This meant high-speed trucks along with steam and signal lines and end buffers.

The truck chassis consisted of a structural-steel platform mounted to the highway truck chassis (straight truck or trailer). This platform included skid rails (to match those on the flatcar) and an adjacent endless conveyor chain driven by a small electric motor, which was powered by the truck's engine. Two key features of the Fitch system were that no crane or lift mechanism was needed, and that the transfer operation could be done by a single person.

To transfer the container, the truck backed to the flatcar so the skid rails were aligned. The driver then connected the anchors, two articulated bridge plates, and two push-pull bars to the flatcar. The plug-in controls included two buttons providing forward and reverse directions for the chain. Forward caused the chain to pull the push-pull bars, pulling the tank from the flatcar to the truck, and vice versa. Stops and limits on the push-pull bars and chassis keep the movement from pulling the tank too far. It took about 90 seconds to transfer the tank from one to the other.

Among the first customers to use the new system on the O&W was Hohneker's Dairy, which shipped tanks from Sherbourne Four Corners, N.Y., to the yard in Weehawken, N.J.—a 235-mile rail trip followed by a 3.5 mile truck transfer to a processing plant in North Bergen, N.J.

Larger tanks

The system worked well, but by 1939 the move was to larger tanks (3,000- and 4,000 gallons), which would quickly become the standard. These larger tanks had additional features compared to the early versions. Along with discharge pipes and plumbing, they included a thermometer, internal agitator, and manway. The initial 4,000-gallon tank, built by Glascote Products Inc., was 20 feet long and had a light weight of 7,300 pounds, making its loaded weight about 41,700 pounds (just over 20 tons).

With these, tanks were now positioned lengthwise on flatcars (up to two to a car), **24**. This time MTI worked with the Pennsylvania Railroad to modify a 70-ton steel flatcar at the railroad's Wilmington, Del., shops. The resulting cars carried MTIX reporting marks. These cars had 10 transverse rails (five per tank) with locking devices at the end of each rail. The significantly longer tanks required semi trailers instead of the straight-chassis trucks of the original design.

The new arrangement required the truck to park parallel to the car for transfer. This simplified truck

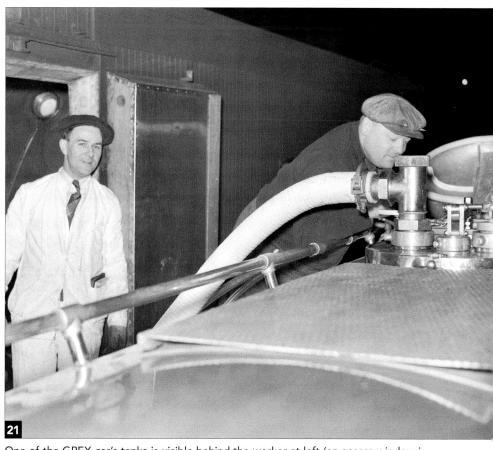

One of the GPEX car's tanks is visible behind the worker at left (an access window is just to the left of his head). The driver has secured the hose to the inlet valve of the truck tank. *Arthur Rothstein, Library of Congress*

A pair of bell-shaped Borden containers on a National Car Co. flatcar are tucked behind the Rutland engine at Alburgh, Vt., in October 1951. *Jim Shaughnessy*

The first milk containers were 8 feet long and mounted transversely on flatcars. These Hohneker's Dairy containers are being unloaded from New York, Ontario & Western flatcar No. 3029. *Motor Terminals Inc.*

The longer 3,000- and 4,000-gallon tanks required side loading. These are publicity photos of Borden tanks on a National Car Co. flat in 1940. *National Car Co.*

In 1934, MDT demonstrated a pair of 2,100-gallon tank trailers on a customized piggyback flatcar equipped for passenger service. *Merchants Despatch*

maneuvering (compared to backing to the car), and was easier to do in the often-narrow spaces available alongside tracks in large yards and team tracks.

The business arrangement for flatcars and milk containers followed the basic guidelines of bulk milk cars, by leasing equipment (flatcars and tanks) to individual dairies and milk companies. Shortly after the move to larger tanks, in early 1940, Fitch, through Motor Terminals, reached an agreement with National Car Company (NCC, itself a subsidiary of Fruit Growers Express)

to form and be the parent of National Fitch Corporation (NFC).

National Fitch acted as the leasing company, while National Car built and provided the railroad equipment. The original O&W cars as well as the Pennsy-modified MTIX cars went into the NCC fleet. This allowed National Car to build and equip flatcars (using FGE and related facilities) and Fitch to supply tanks, with the flatcars having National Car Co. (NX) reporting marks. (The first cars had MTIX marks for Motor Terminals Inc.).

Early customers included Muller Dairies of New York (a division of National Dairy Products Corp.), which in 1939 leased 12 4,000-gallon tanks and nine flatcars; Borden, with an initial agreement in January 1940 to lease 12 3,000-gallon tanks and six flatcars; and Renken Dairy in Brooklyn, which in 1940 leased 14 3,000-gallon tanks and seven flatcars.

The system proved very attractive to the companies with production facilities in New York and New Jersey that were located off-rail, where trucks were required to transport the last few miles from the terminal yard to the plant. For example, Renkin used its initial tanks to haul from various collection creameries in Pennsylvania and New York to the Erie terminal in Jersey City, then used trucks to move the tanks the final few miles to its Brooklyn plant.

An October 1940 article in *Railway Age* reported that more than 50,000 gallons of milk were by that time arriving in New York daily via the Fitch/NCC equipment, and that the number was expected to double by the end of the year.

Although the equipment was initially given AAR class LF (freight) and BMT (passenger), a new AAR car-class designation soon appeared: BMF, specified as a flatcar equipped for passenger service and designed to carry milk bulk containers.

The NCC fleet had 101 flatcars at the peak of operations in 1949, numbered from 1350 to 1499 (not all numbers were used). Cars varied in exact length and specific details. Most were nominal 50-foot cars (most with a 53'-2" overall length), while 19 were 40-footers (nos. 1476, 1480-1499). The 40-foot cars could carry just one larger tank (some still carried multiple small tanks transversely); 50-foot versions carried one or two large tanks.

The tanks were lettered and numbered for their individual lessee. The designs of the tanks varied slightly, with some having flared bases (known as "bell" or "bell-shaped") and others vertical. The access doors and control equipment also varied in style and placement.

In terms of sheer numbers, the

milk container cars carried significant traffic, but never came close to bulk cars in number. However, the cars' appearance is distinctive, and they show up prominently in photos of milk trains on several railroads. Their unique appearance makes them important for modelers.

Borden's was the most notable lessee, with other companies including Hohneker, Muller, Renken, and Sealtest. The cars could appear on any railroad with these companies' dairies on line. Over the years the cars appeared on many railroads, including B&M, DL&W, Erie, LV, NYC, NYO&W, and Rutland. For a time in the mid-1950s as milk service declined, Florida Juice leased several tanks and cars to move its product from Florida to northern markets.

The NCC flatcars were painted black with simple NX reporting marks and number in white, along with "NATIONAL CAR CO." spelled out. The exact placement varied among cars. Tanks wore lettering and paint of the companies that leased them.

The number of NX cars in service declined rapidly by the mid-1950s, with the last cars disappearing from the ORER in 1966. After retirement, some of the tanks were used as stationary tanks at creameries and other businesses; others were scrapped.

Milk piggyback

As Fitch was developing the container system, another similar idea was being put into production by Merchants Despatch: milk tank trailers carried on flatcars in piggyback fashion, **25**. The goal was the same as the milk containers: making it easier for trucks to haul the bulk milk the final miles from rail yards to processing plants without having to transload the product itself.

In the early 1930s, piggybacking was rare but had been done. The Chicago North Shore & Milwaukee was the leader, having carried its own trailers in less-than-carload service for several years, and had also carried common-carrier trailers as well. However, there were no universal standards for equipment or for loading and securing trailers—it was still a developing concept.

The first car for carrying milk trailers on flatcars was built in 1934 by MDT (a patent was filed in 1935 and awarded in 1939). Unlike the North Shore and other operations, which loaded trailers "circus style" at end ramps by backing trailers the length of one or more cars, the milk tanks required a special ramp where the truck backed perpendicular to the car.

The trailer wheels were backed onto a pivoting platform on each end of the car, **26**. Once the trailer's truck tractor was unhitched, the platform was rotated 90 degrees so it was parallel to the car deck. The trailer kingpin was then anchored to a hitch at the center of the car—the trailer hitch mounts were permanent to the car, with braces angling toward the opposite hitch.

By today's standards this seems like a cumbersome operation, but the design eliminated the need for portable jacks that would be used on most piggyback cars into the 1950s (ACF's revolutionary collapsible flatcar trailer hitch was still more than 20 years in the future). The pivoting ramps and hitch anchor did away with tie-down

Trailers were backed perpendicular to the car, then rotated on a platform on the car and locked into place. This was a demonstration of the system in New York City on October 30, 1934. *Merchants Despatch*

chains used on other railroads (some railroads used more than 20 chains on each trailer to secure them)

The trucks were single-axle 2,100-gallon milk tank trailers. The first flatcar, MDT 1500, was a 40-foot car with the same basic construction as the company's contemporary milk cars: a C-channel sideframe, shallow fishbelly center sill, passenger steam and signal lines, high-speed trucks, and end-of-car buffers.

The system was demonstrated in New York City in October 1934, but the idea didn't become popular. The entire fleet would be just three flatcars (1500-1502) and six trailers (200-205), built in 1934 and 1937. Although some remained in service into the 1940s, shippers opted for the container system or standard bulk cars.

The need for a special loading/ unloading ramp was a limiting factor compared to containers, which only required open space at ground level next to the car. The trailer system was also more complex, especially for the mounting and rotating platforms, likely leading to higher maintenance costs. The design also didn't allow for expansion as trailers began growing in size—new, larger trailers would have required a new flatcar design.

The idea was briefly reviewed again in the late 1950s, when piggyback traffic was growing rapidly, with the B&M studying the feasibility of larger trailers. Logistics involving terminal expenses and longer transit times requiring more trailers to cover multiple runs compared to highway trucking kept the idea from coming back.

Demise

The decline in milk traffic through the 1950s led to the eventual retirement of all but the steel-body cars. Some milk tank cars remained in service through the 1960s until the end of rail milk service.

Some GPEX tank cars were repurposed for other commodities, including orange juice, **27**, wine, and vinegar, and some found use in maintenance-of-way service carrying potable water. Most, however, were simply retired and scrapped.

General American-Pfaudler cars (GPEX)			
Number series	Length	Construction	Capacity (gallons)
201-203	40'	wood/steel rebuilt	6,000
501-599	40'	steel rebuilt	6,000
700-800	40'	wood/steel rebuilt	6,000
801-804	40'	steel hooded	7,600
805	40'	Unknown	7,600
807-850	40'	wood/steel rebuilt	6,000
875-880	50'	wood	7,600
881-915	50'	wood	6,000
916-942	40'	steel	6,000
943-944	50'	steel	8,000
945-981	50'	wood	6,000
982-986	50'	steel	6,000
987-1006	40'	steel	6,000
1007-1033	50'	steel	8,000
1034-1045	40'	steel	6,000
1046-1050	50'	steel	8,000
1051-1299	40'	steel	6,000

Not all numbers were used. The specific number of wood and steel cars in service at any given time depended upon rebuilding. Sources: *Railway Milk Cars, Vol. 1*; *Official Railway Equipment Register*, various issues

Summary by type	
40-foot wood	117
50-foot wood	72
40-foot steel	84
50-foot steel	39
Total production:	312 cars

Summary by capacity			
Capacity	1943	1955	1962
6,000	194	160	101
7,600	11	3	1
8,000	2	39	40
Total cars:	207	202	142

Source: *Official Railway Equipment Register*; John Nehrich breakdown by car length; *Railway Milk Cars, Volume 1* (by Robert A. Liljestrand and John Nehrich) includes detailed information for many specific cars, including lessees

By the 1960s, many GPEX cars were out of service or hauling other products. Number 1064 and another 8,000-gallon car are carrying orange juice for Ever Sweet Foods in May 1966. *J. David Ingles*

CHAPTER FIVE

Milk train operations

Milk was carried by train in the U.S. from the 1840s onward. Operations evolved from carrying cans in ordinary boxcars as common freight to cars dedicated to the service carried in passenger trains on tight schedules, **1**. Revenues from these operations kept many milk trains running into the 1950s, when truck competition finally took most milk traffic away.

New York Central 4-8-4 Niagara No. 6000 leads a single MDT reefer and a long string of milk tank and can cars. By the early 1900s, the NYC had become the leading milk-hauling railroad into New York City, with at least four solid trains arriving each day. *New York Central*

How the railroads handled this traffic presents many opportunities for modeling, whether it be single-can operations by local trains or duplicating the tightly scheduled mainline trains and their passenger-train traffic and operations.

First milk operations

Although there are other earlier claims of milk shipments traveling by rail, the first well-documented example came in the spring of 1842. As Chapter 1 described, the bulk of milk sold in New York City at the time was so-called "swill milk," produced by cows kept in the city and fed largely with spent distillers' mash and grain. The milk had an off taste and color, and the conditions in which these cows were kept and milked was often abysmal, but this milk was generally all that was available to most city residents.

A station agent on Erie predecessor New York & Erie, Thaddeus Selleck, had the idea to ship "country" milk (from cows grazed in pastures) produced near Chester, N.Y.—in Orange County about 50 miles north-northwest of Manhattan—into the city via the railroad for sale direct to consumers. Selleck was from New York City, and had worked on the NY&E as it was built through Orange County. While there he sampled some of the local milk, and was taken by the high quality compared to what was

A worker unloads a milk can car, placing cans on a portable gravity conveyor at a milk plant. Each car typically held between 200 and 300 cans, each of which weighed about 113 pounds when full. *U.S. Department of Agriculture*

An A-B set of F3s lead Train 5507, the daily Boston-to-Bellows Falls, Vt., train, returning a mix of empty cars for reloading in 1951. The lead car is a General American-Pfaudler tank leased to Whiting, followed by two Rutland can cars. The fourth and fifth cars are destined for the Bellows Falls creamery, where they will carry cases of bottled milk back to Boston. *S.K. Bolton, Jr.*

Several milk cans await pickup at the Burlington depot in the southwest Iowa town of Clarinda. Farmers often shipped their milk cans by express where volume didn't warrant dedicated milk cars or trains. *Jeff Wilson collection.*

The Milwaukee Road depot at Caledonia, Wis., had a milk platform (right) into the 1920s. The platform was on wheels on rails, and was rolled out to the near track to load cars. *Keith Kohlmann collection*

Dawn is breaking as several farmers load their milk cans into a baggage car from a rural loading platform in Virginia in the early 1900s. *U.S. Department of Agriculture*

available in the city.

Farmers in that area had, to that time, used their milk locally for butter production, and were reluctant to ship their milk what was, at the time, a long distance—the railroad had only been completed a year earlier.

Selleck, however, managed to convince one farmer, Philo Gregory, to ship his milk to the city. One of Gregory's stipulations was that Selleck provide a depot for it as a selling point and to ensure that the quality remained high. Selleck did so, opening a milk depot at 193 Reade Street in Lower Manhattan.

The initial shipment in early 1842 was 240 quarts, which traveled in 60- to 70-quart wooden butter churns. The milk was "refrigerated" by filling tin tubes with ice and inserting them into the containers, which kept the milk from souring. Locals bought the milk by the pail (or other container), which was ladled from the shipping containers.

Buyers noticed the improved quality of the country milk from Chester, and the milk shipments became a daily operation. Selleck quickly found he couldn't keep up with the demand, and soon opened additional depots in the city. The success of the operation and subsequent higher demand led other Orange County farmers to also ship their milk to the city, seeing greater potential for profits than with buttermaking.

The success of this initial milk operation led, the following year, to the first Sunday railroad operations. Until that point, railroads did not operate trains on Sundays. Amid protests from many church groups, the NY&E—which was seeing substantial profits from the daily milk shipments—in 1843 began running Sunday evening trains to carry milk.

By 1847, Orange County farmers were shipping 6 million quarts of milk to the city each year, and other railroads and routes were joining in. Selleck, meanwhile, sold his business in 1844 to the Orange County Milk Association, which continued growing the business.

New York was the country's largest city, and by 1860 had topped a million

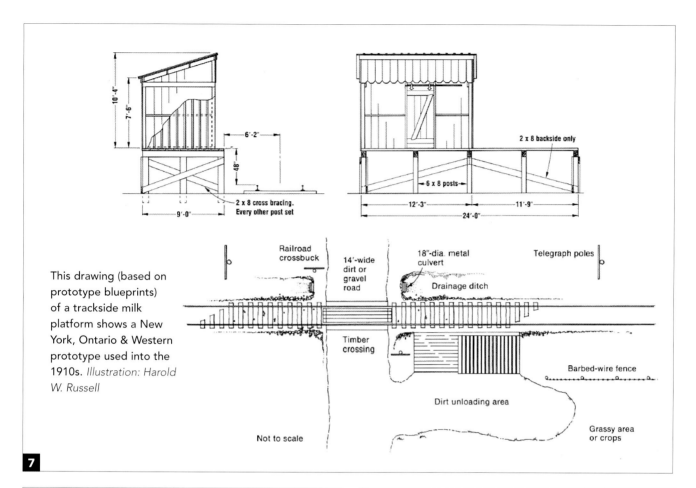

This drawing (based on prototype blueprints) of a trackside milk platform shows a New York, Ontario & Western prototype used into the 1910s. *Illustration: Harold W. Russell*

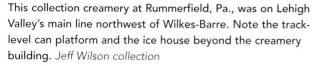

This collection creamery at Rummerfield, Pa., was on Lehigh Valley's main line northwest of Wilkes-Barre. Note the track-level can platform and the ice house beyond the creamery building. *Jeff Wilson collection*

Tank cars were set out the previous day or evening for loading, with precise spotting needed (note the loading pipe). It will be picked up shortly after it's loaded. *New York Central*

in population (including Brooklyn and other boroughs), making it the biggest potential market for inbound milk. It was closely followed by other large cities in the Northeast, including Boston, Philadelphia, Baltimore, and Washington. Rail milk operations to these cities would soon grow to become a large profit center for railroads—albeit one that required a

lot of labor, special equipment, and precise scheduling.

In 1895, railroads carried 8 million 40-quart cans of milk to New York City; by 1915, this had increased to 20 million cans. This meant railroads had to keep reaching farther out from the city to maintain a ready supply of milk, with some routes extending to 500 miles by 1915.

Milksheds

The term "milkshed" refers to the geographical area from which each major city received its milk. The size of the milkshed—and thus the distance milk traveled—varied widely depending upon the size of the city (and thus the demand for milk) and how nearby the dairy farms were that could supply the city's needs.

The Hood's creamery at Sheldon Junction, Vt., had its stub-ended siding on a grade. The train is broken and the car's brakes have been released, which will allow it to roll onto the main. *Philip R. Hastings*

For New York—the nation's largest city—and Boston, for example, most milk came from north and west of the cities, but by the 1900s each had to reach a long distance to get the amount needed. New York's routes spanned up to 500 miles to extreme northern and western New York state and well into Pennsylvania. For Boston, it reached northward to Maine and, for both cities, to the Canadian border in Vermont and New Hampshire. Philadelphia's was 300 miles, reaching westward into Pennsylvania and south through New Jersey and Virginia; Chicago's was also just over 300 miles in the 1930s, reaching northward through Wisconsin and westward across Illinois.

For other cities, the reach was much shorter: 100 miles for Pittsburgh and Cleveland, and just 50 miles for Milwaukee and Minneapolis/St. Paul, so those cities were early to lose rail milk traffic to trucks.

Basic milk operations

Unlike other consumer products traveling by rail, milk was highly perishable. In the days before refrigeration, milk had to be kept as cool as possible and consumed quickly after it was produced. Doing this meant expediting the shipments as much as possible, with the goal usually to have each morning's production bottled later that day or overnight.

Although each railroad handled its milk traffic differently, and likewise each dairy company followed its own guidelines, train and creamery operations followed similar patterns. Trains would leave from the most distant point on the rail line in the morning, picking up milk at platforms and/or creameries along the line until getting to the city. There the cars would either be delivered to creameries, **2**, or loaded onto trucks for final movement to off-line milk plants.

Railroads that did not have direct lines to the large city terminals that they served had to coordinate operations with connecting railroads. An example was the Boston & Maine, which also carried milk from Maine Central, Central Vermont, Rutland, Canadian Pacific, and others into Boston and nearby markets, **3**.

The goal was to get milk delivered, unloaded, cars cleaned (and cans cleaned), and on their way back the evening that they were delivered (or the early morning). Depending upon the length of the route, this meant cars would be ready again for setout and loading on the second or third day after their previous trip.

Typical for the late 1800s into the turn of the century was individual can shipments handled as less-than-carload (LCL) freight. Farmers would bring their cans to a station or trackside loading platform. They would have a ticket for each can (usually bought in advance), with a label tied to the can with the consignee listed—usually a creamery in a larger town or city, **4**. Cans would often be loaded and unloaded from baggage carts, but if milk traffic warranted, a platform might be built, **5**.

Individual farmers might bring in one to a few to a dozen cans; traffic at individual platforms could be anywhere from a handful of cans to a hundred or more (small creameries would also ship via LCL this way, using their own platforms). Farmers would know the train arrival times, and would have to deliver their cans in time to get cans labeled and loaded, **6**. These rural platforms, **7**, were common until about 1910, and could be located near any convenient country road crossing. No spur or siding track was used—the platform would be next to the main, so the train could simply stop, load cans, and go.

These cans would be picked up by trains and—depending upon the level of traffic on a particular route—placed in a baggage car or a dedicated milk car. Railroad personnel would be responsible for getting cars loaded (and for unloading empty cans on reverse routes).

This method of operation continued on low-volume routes until the end of the rail-milk era. Shippers paid LCL rates on cans shipped this way, based on the size of the can used and distance of trip. Cans would be loaded and unloaded by the carrier, and any refrigeration (usually top icing) was done by the carrier.

All LCL was labor-intensive, but milk was even more of a headache. Unlike other LCL shipments, milk cans had to be carried back to the original shipper (farmer or creamery), so they had to be tracked two ways. (Free return was generally part of the ticket price.) Creamery-owned cans typically had the owning company embossed in the can sides or on metal plates affixed to the top shoulder of the can. Cans owned by individual farmers often had letters or numbers painted on the cans; railroads often did this as well, assigning codes to individual stations that received the cans upon return.

As a highly perishable product, milk and cream were vulnerable to spoiling, especially in warm weather or if trains were delayed. This meant the hassle and expense of adding ice atop cans if needed, and dealing with damage claims from milk that had spoiled or soured upon arrival at the consignee.

As traffic increased in volume, railroads began adding cars to trains specifically for carrying milk cans. Early on this usually meant extra baggage-express cars; eventually many railroads built or bought cars just for the traffic as Chapter 3 explains. The range of service was from adding a can car or two to the head-end of a regular passenger train to running a dedicated milk train (perhaps milk and express), with a rider coach or combine tacked on the rear.

Where milk traffic was heavy, small collection creameries began taking the place of multiple small platforms by the early 1900s, **8**. As Chapter 2 explained, these creameries would consolidate the milk from several farmers, and some did additional processing or bottling.

Creameries received the best rates for shipping full carloads (from a single shipper to one consignee). Rates for can cars provided by railroads had a minimum (on the Boston & Maine it was a 200-can minimum for 10-quart cans). This required loading and unloading by the shipper and consignee. Shipping rates varied based on the distance carried. The major markets of New York and Boston had

Wagons of empty cans wait along the milk platform in Washington, D.C., in the early 1900s. Cans were transferred directly across the platform from railcars to wagons or trucks. *U.S. Department of Agriculture*

11

One of New York Central's distinctive can cars awaits reloading with empty cans at a New York City milk platform in 1934. *New York Central*

12

"zones" based on mileage from the cities, with rates based on the zone location of the shipping creamery.

Icing was done by the railroad for cans moving in LCL cars, but shippers were responsible for icing any cars shipped as carload shipments.

For can operations, especially with small creameries or local milk platforms, trains would make many stops, but it was a fairly simple operation with no switching required: The train would stop at the platform, the doors opened, and cans would be loaded in the cars. Most milk trains had a crewman called the "milk messenger"—he, usually with help from creamery workers, would load the car. The doors would then be closed and the train would head to the next stop.

Can operations could be complex, especially for cars filled at multiple stops, as cans could be heading to multiple destinations. This is illustrated well by an example given by John Nehrich in an article in the April 2006 *RailModel Journal*. John cites

a conductor's report from 1952 on the Rutland, with a can car initially loaded at train No. 8's initial station, Ogdensburg, N.Y. More cans were added at two following stops for a total of 226 loaded milk cans. Of these, 122 cans were bound for Boston and 52 for New York City, the two typical destinations for Rutland milk traffic. However, the car also had 15 cans bound for Greenfield, Mass., 14 cans for Worcester, Md., 10 cans each for Keene, N.H., and White River Junction, Vt., and 3 cans for St. Johnsbury, Vt.

Because of this, can cars sometimes needed to be sorted by destination at an intermediate stop. As cars were filled, the cars would be sealed—a seal was applied to the door latch, which was removed at the destination.

Inside the can cars, the cans were lined up on the floors starting at an end. They were kept from sliding during train operations by some type of bar or cable, or by tacking bracing to the floor—photo **3-8** in Chapter

3 shows one such car. The car in that photo has wall-mounted racks that could be folded down atop the first layer of cans to hold a second layer. Many railroads limited cans to a single layer on the floor.

Although most can cars didn't have end ice bunkers, in warm weather the cans would be kept cool by having chunk ice shoveled directly atop them. Blocks of ice could be placed in one end of each car prior to starting their run. The ice would be chopped and shoveled atop cans as they were collected en route. Ice could also be picked up at ice houses and added during the journey.

Larger creameries that loaded full cars of cans would have had cars set out for them the previous day. These would be loaded and (if necessary) iced prior to the train's arrival. Cars shipped as carloads would be sealed by the creamery. This would require switching by the train, as it would have to pick up the car. This also applied to tank cars, which came into wide use by the 1930s and 1940s, **9**.

Bulk transfer required a team track with a clear space for truck parking next to the car. A Dairylea truck collects milk from a 1947-built steel General American-Pfaudler 50-foot car around 1950. *New York Central*

The later the timeframe, the fewer stops made by milk trains, as creameries became larger and farther apart, and those that remained shipped more milk. As an example, in 1930 Dairymen's League had 273 country creameries shipping to the city; by 1936 this had dropped by more than half, to 117.

Instead of stopping quickly to load cans and then moving on, trains had to stop, cut the train, pick up the car or cars, and recouple. This wasn't much different that what a local freight train would do, but because milk cars ran in passenger trains, it typically took a few extra minutes to couple and uncouple cars because of the steam line. This required a trainman to disconnect it (as opposed to the standard air line, which simply pulled apart).

Since most creameries were served by trains heading in both directions (trains picking up loads southbound and dropping off empty cars northbound, for example), many creameries had double-ended tracks

A Belfast & Moosehead Lake GE 70-tonner sets out a General American-Pfaudler tank car at the Hood creamery in Unity, Maine, in 1957. The B&ML interchanged with the Maine Central; rail milk service to the Hood creamery ended in 1959. *B.L. Stone; Krambles-Peterson Archive*

serving them instead of single-ended spurs. This greatly simplified making setouts and pickups.

An option at some creameries was having a single-ended spur on a grade, **10**. The empty would be placed with a

standard trailing-point reverse move. To add the loaded car to the train would ordinarily require the train to run around itself to make a facing-point move. However, with the spur on the grade, the engine would stop and cut off the rear of the train a few car lengths short of the turnout, then pull forward of the turnout.

The brakes on the car would then be released and roll down the spur onto the main line. A brakeman riding the end of the car used the car's end brake wheel to apply the brakes. The engine would then back to the car and the rest of its train, couple up, and be on its way.

Although the same types of cars would tend to show up in the same trains on a daily basis, the exact cars would very. Railroads generally weren't specific about sending the same can cars on the same routes each day. Likewise with tank cars, once cars were cleaned at the terminal and ready to return, the owner or lessee didn't care which specific cars were sent out on which railroad. If three Borden's cars were needed, the next three on the ready track would get pulled.

The major guideline with tank cars, since they were all privately owned or leased, is that they only went to creameries of their owners/lessees. In other words, an H.P. Hood creamery that loaded one tank car a day would only have a Hood car set out at it although the specific cars might vary each day.

Train scheduling

Most milk cars were carried in passenger trains, necessary for the tight scheduling and fast service. Many were secondary passenger trains that also carried express and mail; others were essentially all-milk trains that might have a single rider combine or coach at

15 Eastbound Boston & Maine Train 58, the *Minute Man*, has three milk tank cars and a can car trailing 4-6-2 No. 3658 as it approaches North Pownal, Vt., in August 1940. *John P. Ahrens*

the rear, or that wouldn't take revenue passengers.

Way freight or mixed trains often picked up loads and dropped off empties on branch lines, leaving cars at junction points for pickup by milk trains. Multiple trains would sometimes pick up milk cars along various stretches of main line, dropping off milk cars at key towns. This allowed a long-distance milk train to make fewer stops along its route.

Many milk train schedules were, overall, not fast, but this had to account for the multiple stops that had to be made, and most had a bit of padding in their schedules to allow for minor delays along the way. All operating personnel knew that milk trains' schedules had to be met and trains were not to be delayed—even moreso than many passenger trains. A delayed passenger might become upset, but wasn't in danger of spoiling.

This was especially true for cars that would be handed off for other train connections or railroads, and for interchanging entire trains to another

railroad. The connecting train may wait for a brief time, but this depended upon the number of cars and the specific schedule.

In setting schedules, railroads usually wanted trains to arrive at their city terminals from late evening into early morning—spreading out delivery times among trains, but allowing time for that evening's arriving milk to be bottled for delivery the following morning. This had to be balanced against departure times in the farthest outlying towns, giving creameries enough time to have cans and cars loaded and ready for trains.

Distance and time were then balanced in setting schedules. In a rate testimony session in 1915 before the New York State Senate, it was defined that the goal of the railroads should be to get milk from its collection point to the city in 16 hours or less, "in such a condition as will meet the requirements of public health."

Any number of problems could waylay trains and keep them from making their schedules. Creameries not having cars loaded and ready on time could be a serious issue. Late cars and those that missed connections might be picked up by a following train, which might then be expedited. This was less a problem on some high-capacity lines which hosted multiple milk (or other high-priority) trains, but could be a severe concern for a route that had all milk traffic in a single passenger train.

Milk cars had high-speed trucks, but they were still equipped with solid bearings (wide use of roller bearings was still some years away). These had journal boxes at the ends of the axles, with a cloth pad or ball of cotton waste impregnated with oil to keep the bearings lubricated. If the bearings ran dry, the result was a hotbox.

Needless to say, car inspectors kept a close eye on milk cars, making sure journal boxes were lubricated and cars were in good repair. A hotbox or other breakdown could mean having to reload a carload of cans (or transload a bulk load) to another railcar or to trucks.

Derailments, wrecks, engine failures, and weather issues were always possible. Railroads would have to re-route cars if needed, or in extreme cases, call on trucks to carry the milk if a delay would be excessive.

Dispatchers would give every advantage to milk trains to get them to their connection or terminal on time, and had to work to minimize delays whenever possible. Milk cars required priority handling at interchanges, yards, and terminals.

Transfer operations

A challenge for operations in New York City, Boston, and New Jersey was that most of the large city production plants were located off line—often a few miles from the nearest rail yard or siding. This required milk to be transferred from railcars to trucks, whether carried in cans or tanks.

Through the 1920s, these terminals had long trackside platforms at car-floor height, **11**. For can cars, when a train arrived at a terminal, the cars were spotted along the platform. Trucks of the receiving dairy companies would already be waiting for the trains' arrivals. Workers at the docks opened the cars and begin moving the cans across the platform, where they would be loaded into trucks and on their way, **12**.

By the 1930s, operations were trending toward tank cars and tank containers (see Chapter 4). These required a track with a clear drive area next to it, **13**. From this period into the 1960s, milk platforms as well as team track areas were needed to transfer milk.

Routes by railroad

Let's take a look at how basic traffic was handled on several major milk-hauling railroads. There isn't enough space to include listings of all creameries and shippers—much less all railroads and trains—on each route. Specific trains (and train numbering) and schedules/timing changed over the years, sometimes dramatically.

Many major railroads also interchanged milk cars with various short lines, including Maine's Belfast & Moosehead Lake, **14**, St. Johnsbury & Lamoille County in Vermont, the Huntington & Broad Top in

16 Central Vermont 2-8-0 No. 465 leads a long milk train southbound out of Montpelier Junction, Vt., in June 1949. The first car is a GPEX tank leased to Whiting; the second, fourth, and fifth cars are CV can cars. *John P. Ahrens*

Pennsylvania, and the Unadilla Valley in New York.

Much information of specific operations involving milk traffic have been lost to time. For some railroads, a lot of information has been published in books or historical society magazines; for others, not so much. This available information is not always in proportion to the milk quantity carried by each railroad.

Railroad-specific books and historical society publications and websites are often good sources for detailed information on specific shippers, volume of shipments, types of cars used, and specific trains that handled traffic. Check the bibliography on page 94 as a starting point.

Boston & Maine

The Boston & Maine was the major railroad providing milk deliveries to Boston, both collected from its own routes as well as connections with other railroads (about 60 percent of Boston's milk deliveries in 1948), **2**. The B&M had routes out of Boston north along the coast to Portsmouth; a longer route up to Portland and a connection with Maine Central; northwestern routes to White River Junction, Vt. (interchange with the Central Vermont), Woodsville, N.H. (interchange with Canadian Pacific), Bellows Falls, Vt. (junctions with CV and Rutland); and a western line to the Troy-Albany, N.Y., area (Delaware & Hudson interchange at Eagle Bridge, N.Y.), **15**.

By the 1940s and 1950s, the vast majority of this traffic was in tank cars. In 1956 tank cars totaled 71 percent (10,393 cars), followed by can cars (17 percent, 2,483 cars), then "bottle cars" (10 percent, 1,498 cars), with the rest single cans in baggage cars. The bottle cars handled cases of bottled milk from the Bellows Falls Cooperative Creamery to First National Stores in Boston.

H.P. Hood was the major milk supplier in the Boston market. By 1956, Hood received cars from 37 country stations: 30 shipping tank cars and 7 shipping can cars. Of those, the top shippers for tank cars were Salem, N.H., (906 cars) and West Farmington, Maine (728 cars);

Delaware & Hudson 4-6-2 No. 602 gets set to roll southward out of Whitehall, N.Y., with a milk train in August 1947. Behind the engine are wood and steel tank cars followed by milk containers on a flatcar. *Bert Pennypacker*

Lackawanna Train 27 hauls a long train of empty milk cars westward between Foster and Kingsley, Pa., including several of DL&W's distinctive can cars, milk containers on flatcars, and Borden "butter dish" cars. *Wayne Brumbaugh*

for can cars, Newport Junction, Me., shipped 605 cars and St. Albans, Vt., 406 cars. Whiting received cars from six stations, with the top ones shipping just over 350 cars.

Boston can cars terminated at the milk platform in Somerville, and tank cars at their respective dairies. Not all loaded milk cars went to Boston proper. Although 78 percent of tank cars went to Boston, 18 percent went to Lynn, Mass., and the rest to Lawrence, Mass. For can cars, 72 percent went to Boston, about 6 percent each to Providence, R.I., and Hartford, Conn., and the rest to other locations.

B&M train 5500 carried traffic out of Bellows Falls (at 9:05 p.m.) to Somerville. Along with other interchange traffic, the Bellows Falls Co-op generated significant traffic—in 1963, 1.6 million cases, or 1,857 total carloads. The creamery was actually on the Rutland, which switched the creamery and immediately handed cars

to the B&M. The train ran through 1964, when a Massachusetts state law began requiring bottled milk sold in the state be bottled there. Whiting was awarded the new contract, and this service—and the need for B&M's unique mechanically refrigerated bottle cars—ended.

Other key trains included a daily (except Saturday) milk extra from White River Junction and an East Deerfield Extra for the Eagle Bridge, N.Y., traffic. Maine Central traffic from the Portland Division came down on B&M train RB-2 (from Portland's Rigby Yard).

Central Vermont

The Central Vermont ran from the northern border of Vermont and a connection with parent Canadian National southward through Vermont, Massachusetts, and Connecticut to a connection with the New York, New Haven & Hartford at New London. This gave it connections to

both Boston and New York, but no direct access. The line used a stretch of trackage rights on Boston & Maine south of White River Junction, Vt.

On the Northern Division (north of White River Junction), local trains picked up loads at creameries, which were then picked up by through trains at Essex Junction or Montpelier Junction. Milk was handled by mixed train No. 210 (southbound) and 211 (north). By the 1950s, milk headed south on 510 (490 on Saturday), **16**, with northbound empties on 511 (429 Sundays).

Most milk from the CV went to Boston via the B&M interchange at White River Junction. The CV was second in supplying milk to that city only to B&M as of 1956.

Delaware & Hudson

The D&H stretched from northern New York (Rouses Point at the Canadian border) and a connection with Canadian Pacific to Montreal,

downward to Albany (and interchange with New York Central and with Boston & Maine at nearby Eagle Bridge), then west to Binghamton, N.Y., and Scranton and Wilkes-Barre, Pa, **17**.

Milk was shipped as express until 1893, with most traveling southwest to Binghamton and transferring to the Erie. By 1899, there was a milk train picking up loads from Binghamton to Albany, handing off to the New York Central.

In 1904, milk began arriving from north of Albany for shipment to New York, growing to 50 cars a day by the mid-1920s. This traffic was handled by Train 18, which started at dawn at Rouses Point as a combined southbound milk and passenger train. At Whitehall, N.Y., the passenger cars were separated and continued as local train No. 4. The milk cars were combined with cars from train No. 20.

Number 20 had left Colonie Yard (on the north side of Albany) and was unique in that it both made setouts of empties and pickups of loaded cars as it headed east on the Rutland and Washington branch, to Eagle Bridge, then up the branch to Castleton, Vt., and back westward to Whitehall.

The combined train (as No. 20) then headed back down to Green Island (Troy), where the New York Central picked up the cars and carried them to New York City down its Hudson Division. Most empties returned north on 3 (4's counterpart).

The D&H's peak milk shipments were in 1931, then traffic fell dramatically. Train 18 was discontinued in 1954.

Delaware, Lackawanna & Western

The Lackawanna was a major supplier of milk to New York City from the late 1800s onward, ranking first for a time in 1900. Its line extended from Hoboken, N.J., northwest through Pennsylvania to Binghamton, N.Y. In 1900, four eastbound mainline trains from Binghamton carried milk: nos. 42 (departing Elmira, N.Y., at 8:10 a.m.), followed by 44, 46, and 48 (with

Empty milk cars return westward on Erie Train 9 near Oxford, N.Y., in May 1945. Behind the engine are tank cars still sporting signboards for Alderney Dairy and Dairymen's League. *Donald W. Furler*

empties returning on westbound nos. 41, 43, 45, and 47), **18**. They were also fed by trains 811 from DL&W's branch to Syracuse and 848 from the Richfield Springs branch (which extended northeast from Binghamton). The mainline trains also carried mail and express, and 42 and 43 had a rider coach. Numbers 41 and 48 were eliminated in the 1910s.

The Lackawanna's milk trains terminated at the milk terminal in Hoboken, with some cars dropped at Passaic, N.J. Number 42 arrived at 8:35 p.m.; 44 and 46 about two hours later. Upon arrival, a switcher took the passenger and express cars away, then moved the milk cars to team tracks (tank cars) or the milk platform (can cars), where wagons and trucks were waiting. The milk cars were then cleaned, and cleaned and sterilized cans and bottles returned to their cars, where they were reassembled into Train 43, due out at 3:30. Other empty trains followed shortly.

Hoboken's main platform was 1,200 feet long; some cars were forwarded to Newark and Montclair. The DL&W also carried milk from Sussex County, N.J., to Orange and Newark.

Traffic peaked around 1930, with Dairymen's League the railroad's largest milk shipper, followed by Borden and Sheffield Farms. Train 43 was discontinued in 1929, 42 in 1940,

and 45 and 46 in 1933. Trains 44/47 ran until the Erie-Lackawanna merger in 1960, mostly carrying tank cars to Orange and Newark. The last shipment (on EL) came in 1966 from Sheffield Farms in Homer, N.Y.

Erie
The Erie was the first to ship milk to New York City (in 1842), and by 1847 was operating a regular milk train. Its main line extended west to Binghamton, Elmira, and Hornell, N.Y., plus branches. By 1897 milk was being brought to the city (the milk terminal at Jersey City) from Hornellsville, N.Y. (331 miles); by 1915 it was coming as far as South Dayton, N.Y. (448 miles).

By the 1910s, Erie ran several milk trains: from Salamanca, N.Y. (413 miles distant), leaving at 7:30 a.m. and arriving at Jersey City at 11:55 p.m.; from Susquehanna, Pa., leaving at 10:50 a.m. and arriving at 10:15 p.m.; and from Pine Island, N.Y., leaving at 4 p.m. and arriving at 9:20 p.m. (picking up Lehigh & Hudson River traffic as well), and from Walwick, N.Y., which also handled LCL traffic. Other trains fed these trains from branches; all picked up from various connections en route.

By the 1940s, most milk was being carried on Train 28, which left Binghamton at 11:05 a.m. and

arrived in Jersey City at 7:25 p.m., and Train 8 (the *Atlantic Express*), which left Binghamton at 5:51 p.m. and arrived in Jersey City at 11:40 p.m. Empties returned on trains 9 (leaving Jersey City at 11:00 a.m., arriving Binghamton at 6:15 p.m.), **19**, and 27, the *Mountain Express* (out of Jersey City at 3:40 p.m., arriving in Binghamton at 9:10 p.m.). The *Erie Limited* and *Midlander/Lake Cities* occasionally carried milk cars, but it was not a frequent occurrence.

The Erie delivered inbound milk cars at Pavonia Avenue in Jersey City, near the passenger station. The milk terminal had five platforms that could handle 60 cars.

Lehigh Valley
The Lehigh Valley extended west from New York City into Pennsylvania, then turned northward through Wilkes-Barre, Sayre, Pa., and into New York through Geneva and to Buffalo. Multiple branches in central New York extended through Ithaca to Camden,

20 Lehigh Valley had a saddle-tank 0-6-0 switcher at Sayre, Pa., in the 1930s. In the background at left are LV's distinctive wood, archbar-truck milk cars, plus (at right) two first-generation General American milk cars (both owned by Sheffield Farms, SFCX). *Frank Snyder*

Auburn, and to North Fair Haven on Lake Ontario.

By the 1890s, milk from these branches was funneled by multiple trains to Sayre, picked up by locals, **20**, and from there consolidated and taken to New York. In 1897 the LV's longest milk haul was 335 miles; by 1915, the longest run was from Camden, N.Y., 400 miles.

In 1901, LV hauled 49,922 tons of milk and cream, the equivalent of 1.16 million 10-gallon cans, or 3,180 cans per day.

As of 1915, LV ran two long-distance milk trains, one from North Fair Haven, 386 miles from Jersey City, and another from Canastota, N.Y. (382 miles). The North Fair Haven train departed at 7:50 a.m., arrived at Sayre at 1:30, and picked up cars collected by other trains. It arrived at 3:30 at Tunkhannock, Pa., picking up more cars, and was due at Jersey City at 10:30 p.m. The Canastota train started at 9:15 a.m., and arrived at Jersey City at 11 p.m. The LV also ran what was called the Jersey Little Milk Train, with about five cars, running from Easton, Pa., collecting milk produced in New Jersey.

Inbound milk arrived at Warren Street at Jersey City, a milk platform with a 24-car capacity; Avenue B (4 cars); and Pioneer Street in Newark (5 cars). All were strictly milk terminals. Empty cars from the two long-distance trains are returned in one train (no. 37) to Sayre, **21**, where several trains redistributed them.

Maine Central

The Maine Central covered its namesake state with a web of lines branching outward from its southern terminus at Portland, Me. One line headed west and north to St. Johnsbury, Vt., and north to the Canadian border; other lines headed north and east across the state.

Most creameries along the MEC were owned or controlled by Hood, with some by Whiting and an earlier company, Turner Centre, which was acquired by Hood in 1928. Hood acquired the Whiting creameries as well in 1946. Cans were carried in the MEC's insulated boxcars, but Hood switched to bulk cars for most shipments by the 1940s, **22**. Along with its own traffic, the MEC forwarded a few cars from the Bangor & Aroostook as well.

Train 163 brought milk cars from the western (Mountain Division) line to Portland. From the east, milk came on trains 12, 24 (from Farmington), and 48 (from Bangor). Loads were interchanged at Portland to the Boston & Maine, which brought them southward on various trains.

New York Central

By the early 1900s, the New York Central carried more milk into New York City than any other railroad, **1**. This included milk from NYC's own lines as well as movements from Delaware & Hudson, Rutland, and others, coming in via the railroad's Hudson, Harlem, and West Shore

A single rider coach trails 17 assorted empty milk cars (and container cars) returning westbound on Lehigh Valley Train 37. Pacific No. 2030 leads the train at Falls, Pa., in this undated photo. *W.R. Osborne*

A combine trails three H.P. Hood milk tank cars on a Maine Central train as it passes the ball signals at Coos Junction, N.H. *Trains magazine collection*

lines. The railroad had many notable milk trains—keep in mind that specific connections, assignments, and train numbers evolved over the years. Here's a summary of key trains:

Number 180 started at Syracuse at 11:15 a.m. (as of 1915) with cars from several branches. It picked up cars from multiple stations, cars from the St. Lawrence Division (from Trains 20 and 16, which originated in Massena, N.Y.), then ran through to Rensselaer to be combined with cars from the D&H, then to New York. Empties returned on Train 181. Train 186 picked up cars from Black River (Train 64) in western New York, then at Herkimer, N.Y., including cars from the Poland branch, then on to Rensselaer.

Train 184 was the combined 70 and 64. Train 70 left Watertown, N.Y., usually with about 14 cars, preceded by a milk extra (local), then combined with Train 64 off the Utica-Carthage

branch at Utica. The train picked up cars from Ogdensburg-Utica train No. 570. Known as the Big Milk, this train sometimes ran in two sections with up to 50 cars, running through from Utica on the Hudson Division to New York City. Most cars went to the 60th Street milk yard, but some were dropped off at Bronx Terminal Market and 130th Street Yard (the train was due just before midnight).

Train 188 left Syracuse at 8:41 a.m., picked up five or six cars along West Shore (and also some freight), and continued to Rensselaer Yard. Its milk cars were combined with those off the D&H; the train then headed to New York on the Hudson Division as Train 182, due at 60th Street Yard at 12:20 a.m. Empties headed back on Train 793, departing at 2:45 a.m., with D&H-bound cars leaving on Train 183 at 5:30 a.m. and St. Lawrence Division empties on 185 at 8:30 a.m.

Through the mid-1950s, the Rutland delivered a trainload of cars to the NYC at Chatham, N.Y., each evening at 9 p.m. This continued on the NYC as Train 88 down the Harlem Division, dropping cars at Bronx Terminal and 130th Street before arriving at 60th Street at 3:20 a.m. Empties from this train departed for Chatham at 1 p.m. as Train 77 to meet the arriving southbound loaded Rutland train.

Train 528 from Oneonta handled milk and express. It traveled to New York via Kingston, coming down the West Shore to Weehawken, N.J.

Capacity of the 130th Street platforms was 40 cars; at 33rd Street, 32 cars (three tracks); and at 60th Street, 87 cars (10 tracks).

By the 1940s, the Central carried about 40 percent of city's total milk, with about 75 percent arriving by tank car and the rest in cans. Milk traffic dropped dramatically by the mid-

1950s and was gone by the 1960s.

New York, Ontario & Western

The NYO&W ran north and west from Weehawken, N.J. (with trackage rights on the West Shore, later the New York Central, to Cornwall, N.Y.), then to Oswego, N.Y., with another line splitting at Cadosia, N.Y., and dropping south to Scranton, Pa.

Milk was a major portion of the railroad's traffic into the 1930s, and the railroad began regular milk trains into the New York City market (Weehawken) in 1871. As the New York milkshed expanded, the O&W's milk runs became longer. In 1881 the railroad shipped a carload of milk 195 miles from Delhi, N.Y., to New York City, and by 1892 milk was arriving from Oneida, N.Y. By 1902 the O&W was the largest milk supplier to New York, providing an eighth of the city's total. Milk arrived at the Weehawken terminal, which by 1916 had five platforms (four used by O&W, the other by a NYC West Shore train).

By the early 1900s, the railroad had two main eastbound milk trains: No. 10, known as the Long Milk, which

left Oneida (on the line to Oswego) at 8:15 a.m. It made mainline stops and picked up cars from several branches (Rome, train No. 182; Utica, No. 60; and New Berlin, No. 174). Train 12, the Short Milk, started at Walton (just north of Cadosia) and picked up local milk and cars from the Delhi branch as well as the Scranton Division. The two trains combined at Cornwall and ran to Weehawken as No. 10, arriving just before 9 p.m. Specific assignments varied over the years, and by the 1920s, No. 10 was leaving Oswego and No. 12 from Sidney.

The railroad's milk traffic peaked in the mid-1920s, then began to drop dramatically—as did its other traffic, **23**. The railroad struggled financially and with low traffic levels, and in 1957 ceased operations.

Pennsylvania Railroad

The Pennsy carried a good deal of milk traffic, mainly into Philadelphia (23.4 million gallons in 1915). It didn't carry milk to New York until 1913, but began doing so on train BF10, originating at East Aurora, N.Y., (about 500 miles distant) at 8 a.m. and

Traction companies

Interurban (electric) lines also carried milk into some cities. This could be done as regular LCL traffic, or in dedicated cars. Just after the turn of the 20th century, the Eastern Ohio Traction Company was carrying up to 6,000 gallons (600 cans) of milk per day into Cleveland, with 10,000 gallons arriving via electric railway each day. In 1914, the (electric) Detroit United Railway carried 2,000 cans daily into the city.

Philadelphia in 1915 saw 1.78 million gallons of milk carried to the city by electric lines. The Philadelphia & West Chester had a milk platform at 63rd and Market streets in Philadelphia, where cans would be transferred from its cars to wagons and trucks each morning.

Most of this traffic comprised cans picked up from multiple platforms along the routes. Interurbans, because of their generally short routes, were among the first to lose milk traffic as roads and streets improved. Most of this business was gone by the 1920s.

Three milk cars—an early General American tank car and two flatcars with milk containers—are at the head of a New York, Ontario & Western train near New Berlin Junction (between Sidney and Norwich, N.Y.) in June 1946. The locomotive is 2-8-0 No. 307. *H.D. Runey*

arriving at Jersey City at 12:15 a.m. and at Flatbush Avenue in Brooklyn at 1 a.m. The Pennsy's milk traffic wasn't always highly visible, as the railroad mainly used its ubiquitous R50b express reefers (it had 500 of them), plus earlier B50 and B50a cars, for can shipments. Most online milk shipments moved in tank cars by the 1940s, **24**.

Milk was largely carried on secondary passenger trains, with locals making pickups and deliveries at creameries. From New York, Train 69 (the *Red Arrow*) carried empties west from to Harrisburg and Altoona, locals handled delivery and pickup,

and loaded milk came back on No. 74, the *Duquesne*. In the 1920s and 1930s, symbol train RA from Renovo, Pa., to Jersey City, carried solid blocks of milk cars (often more than 25).

Out of Philadelphia, Train 19 (later 35) would carry empties to Huntington, Pa., with Train 8 (later 96 and 612) carrying them back to Philly. Milk and other products also traveled on Trains D16 and D17 from Delmar, Del., to Philadelphia via Wilmington, and on MD58 and MD59 from Perryville, Md.

Reading Co.
The Reading carried milk to

Philadelphia from its lines that extended west past Harrisburg to Gettysburg, Pa., notably from the railroad's Lebanon Valley branch. Loads were carried by eastbound Train GP2, which left Gettysburg at 1:30 p.m., reaching Reading at 8 p.m. and the milk terminal in Philadelphia just before midnight. Empties were returned by overnight Train 81, which left Philadelphia at 1:30 a.m. and arrived at Reading at 4:30 a.m. The train then became Train 149 for run to Harrisburg, arriving there at 6:45 a.m. and Gettysburg at 9 a.m.

By the 1940s this traffic had largely

moved to trucks, and the Reading's milk trains were eliminated.

Rutland

The Vermont-based Rutland supplied milk to both New York City and Boston, and was a major carrier. In 1936 the line carried 2.09 million loaded milk cans—an average of 5,719 per day, **25**.

The railroad looks like an inverted "Y," coming down the state from the north at Alburgh with a western branch extending to Ogdensburg, N.Y. The line splits at Rutland, with one line heading southwest to Chatham, N.Y., and a connection with the New York Central (to New York City) and the other line heading southeast to Bellows Falls and a Boston & Maine connection to carry milk to Boston.

In the 1910s, the line's milk train departed Ogdensburg in the early morning as train No. 8, then became 88 when it turned south at Alburgh, collecting milk en route. The train arrived in Rutland in late afternoon. About a quarter of the milk cars then headed for Bellows Falls (Boston),

with a crew-only combine (as local No. 156 until the train was discontinued in 1948). From there, the cars left on B&M Train 5500, leaving Bellows Falls at 9:05 p.m. and arriving overnight at Somerville, just short of Boston's North Station.

The B&M returned empty cars on 5509, and they usually were picked up on the Rutland by the *Mount Royal*, the railroad's overnight passenger train. The *Royal* would often carry the empties at the rear of the train to make switching the head-end mail easier.

The rest of the milk headed from Rutland south to Chatham as Train 56. Upon arrival at Chatham, loaded cars were switched to the NYC, which took it down the Harlem Division as NYC Train 88, arriving overnight.

The Central's return train on the Harlem was 77. The Rutland crew handing off 56 had about a 90 minute wait, then the NYC dropped off empties and the Rutland train headed north (basically a "turn") as 83, then became 87, then 7 upon leaving Alburgh for Ogdensburg. In warm

weather, no. 7 would pause at the ice house at Alburgh, where blocks of ice were loaded into the empty can cars for use atop cans the following morning.

When Rutland employees went on strike in the summer of 1953, one side effect was the discontinuance of passenger trains once operations resumed. Milk then had to be handled in freight trains.

By the 1950s, more milk headed to Bellows Falls than Chatham; this was complete after 1957 with a Federal order cutting Vermont out of the New York milkshed. Overall milk traffic was dropping dramatically, and all service on the Rutland shut down in 1961 following a strike.

Central and Midwestern operations

Several central and Midwestern cities received milk by rail, including Detroit, Cincinnati, Cleveland, Indianapolis, Milwaukee, and Minneapolis-St. Paul. Most, however, were handled by can traffic in regular trains, with trucks taking over most business by the 1930s.

24 Pennsylvania Train 21, the *Keystone Express*, carries an MDT-built Supplee car (with MILK and ICE CREAM lettering) at the head end at the Lancaster, Pa., station in July 1935. *Warren W. McCleary*

Rutland 2-6-0 No. 57 gets ready to lead an extra with four milk tank cars at the head end out of Brandon, Vt., in 1945.
J.H. Williams

By far the greatest rail-based milk traffic outside of the Northeast was the Chicago area. It developed much later than that of New York or Boston, as the area wasn't settled as soon and the population wasn't as dense.

Chicago milk traffic

Chicago's population was growing rapidly in the late 1800s. The city grew from just under 300,000 residents in 1870 (the country's fifth-largest city) to 1.1 million in 1890 and 1.7 million by 1900, making it the second-largest U.S. city behind New York.

The increased food demands of the population, plus the city's location as the gateway and grand junction for eastern and western railroads, put Chicago in a good position for receiving milk by rail. Most milk consumed in the city was produced to the north and west: from northeast Illinois counties (including nearby McHenry, which ranked third in the country in milk production behind New York's St. Lawrence and Orange counties) and from southeastern Wisconsin running northward along Lake Michigan up to Door County. Some milk also came by rail from

the south and east (Michigan and Indiana).

According to a 1913 report from the U.S. Department of Agriculture, most of Chicago's milk supply at that time was produced within 60 miles of the city (75 percent in Illinois), with 100 miles being the extent of most milk runs (extending in times of peak demand to 200 miles). The short runs for most of this traffic meant most traveled in ordinary baggage cars, with trains setting out from outbound terminals around 6 a.m. and cars delivered in the city by noon. Empties were then on their way back by afternoon. This was faster than most Eastern milk runs.

Chicago statistics show 8-gallon (32-quart) cans, which apparently were more common in the area than the 10-gallon variety favored elsewhere (see "Chicago Milk Traffic" on page 88).

Chicago was served by dozens of small bottling plants and dealers, with the market not dominated by major companies as in the East. Many small operations would simply buy a few cans of milk from brokers each day and bottle them in backroom or garage operations.

Chicago was also surrounded by numerous country bottling plants, served by local farmers. At these, milk brought in the morning was pasteurized and bottled that day, then shipped by rail or truck into the city for delivery the following morning. These companies pushed the ideals of "milk bottled in the country," as opposed to milk brought to Chicago and bottled there.

By 1930, Chicago's population had tripled from the turn of the century, to 3.38 million. This meant increased milk consumption, so although many short milk routes had been taken over by trucks, some rail routes by the mid-1930s extended more than 330 miles—notably to northern Wisconsin on the Chicago & North Western, Wisconsin Central (Soo Line), and Milwaukee Road. Other lines still carrying milk (most in baggage cars) included the Pennsy, Monon, Rock Island, Milwaukee Road, Chicago Great Western, and Erie.

The move to tank cars in the area took place early, with the first three Wieland cars in 1922 followed by cars for Bowman in 1924, **26**. By 1931 Bowman had 40 cars in service and

Borden-Wieland 26 cars, along with other General American-Pfaudler cars leased to smaller companies, including Freeport Milk Products, Interstate Creameries, Lemont Dairy, Ira J. Mix Dairy, Marley Dairy, Merkle Dairy, White Eagle Dairy, Western Dairy, Selios Brothers Dairy, and others.

On the Chicago & North Western by 1900, dedicated can trains would arrive from the Galena Division (sometimes in two sections) and Wisconsin Division, with cans picked up at stations all along the route—5,500 cans per day at the turn of the century. Most were from individual farmers. They would buy tickets (usually in bulk) in advance, and affix the tickets to their cans, each of which is labeled for themselves and their station stop, and each of which is bound for a specific consignee in the city.

Inbound trains arrived at Chicago's Clinton Street milk platform at 10:15 a.m., where wagons and trucks were waiting. The platform handled 2 million cans in 1900 and more than 4 million in 1910.

Milk traffic dropped off by the 1930s, but some can traffic continued later in standard passenger and express trains, **27**, with more traveling by tank car.

On the Wisconsin Central, milk was originally handled by a local, but as of 1888, the WC began operating milk train No. 10. It departed Waukesha, Wis. (just west of Milwaukee) at 5:55 a.m. and made the nearly 100-mile trek to Chicago in just under four hours, arriving at 9:50. The train stopped at milk platforms en route, spaced about every 10 miles apart. Farmers left their cans at the platforms, buying tickets as with the C&NW.

The Soo leased the WC in 1909 and extended service beyond Waukesha to Lomira, 142 miles from Chicago, and eventually reached even farther. The railroad shipped 261,000 cans by 1892 and about 300,000 by 1910.

Can traffic was dropping by the 1920s, with the milk train making its last run in 1922 and train No. 7 picking up remaining traffic. Individual

A Chicago-area milk strike in 1935 (over milk pricing) led to picketers blocking inbound trucks and trains and dumping milk, as with this early Bowman tank car on the Chicago & North Western near Genoa City, Wis. *Jeff Wilson collection*

Two Chicago-bound milk cars are tucked behind the locomotive at left at Appleton Junction, Wis., in the 1940s. *A.C. Kalmbach*

This colorized image from around 1900 shows wagons carrying tubs of butter from the Milaca, Minn., co-op creamery to a team track for loading in a Great Northern reefer. The butter is heading to Northeast markets. *Jeff Wilson collection*

A Merchants Despatch refrigerator car is being loaded with butter at the Remus, Mich., creamery. The brick construction is typical of small Midwestern creameries. *Jeff Wilson collection*

Chicago milk traffic

Railroad	1900	1910
Average number of 8-gallon cans by railroad per day		
Chicago & North Western	6,000	12,200
Milwaukee Road	3,500	8,600
Illinois Central	1,500	1,775
Chicago Great Western	1,200	1,400
Wisconsin Central (Soo)	700	800
Burlington Route	700	800
Rock Island	500	600
Santa Fe	500	300
Grand Trunk	400	500
Pennsylvania	400	500
Erie	300	620
Wabash	300	300
Total:	*20,125	*31,245
*Not all railroads listed		

farmers were instead bringing their cans to collection creameries or cheese processing plants. Milk platforms along the line were removed by the early 1930s, with remaining traffic handled at stations. The Milwaukee Road handled traffic in much the same manner.

Finished-product operations

As Chapter 2 explained, not all milk produced gets bottled and sold as milk or cream. A large percentage goes to make other products, mainly butter, cheese, evaporated and condensed milk, and powdered milk. These products were shipped by truck and rail, and unlike raw milk itself, some of these finished products are still shipped by rail.

Creameries and production plants shipped these products to a variety of destinations, including supermarket chains, baking companies, food processing plants, and wholesalers and brokers. The U.S. government has also bought a great deal of finished goods as well.

The Midwest produced most of the country's butter (the top four states in the 1920s were Minnesota, Wisconsin, Iowa, and Ohio) in the early 1900s, and most of it was consumed in the Northeast. This meant cars loaded in the Midwest and plains states and headed eastward.

Most of this went in standard refrigerator cars. Butter was perishable and needed to be kept cool, but it had a long shelf life compared to raw milk.

Shipping time, therefore, wasn't critical, so butter usually traveled in standard freight reefers. Creameries got the best shipping rates for full carloads. In the early 1900s, many Midwestern creameries formed co-ops to make it easier to consolidate butter to large shipments to get better rates, **28**.

By the 1920s and '30s, creameries were becoming larger as truck-pickup routes allowed expanded coverage areas. More creameries also had on-site cold storage with mechanical refrigeration, allowing butter to be stored until there was enough to ship entire carloads (or wait for better prices). A small creamery might ship out a refrigerator car of butter once every week or two; larger operations, more frequently.

These creameries present great modeling opportunities, as they were located throughout the central, Midwest, and plains states, and many were in small towns, **29**. These could also get incoming rail shipments, such as packaging (butter tubs, crates) and salt, which could arrive by truck as well. As **2-27** shows, railroads are still carrying dairy products, although mainly from larger operations that generate multiple carloads.

1

CHAPTER SIX

Milk and dairy trucks

Trucks have carried milk and milk products since internal-combustion engines were first applied to wagons. These range from trucks designed to carry milk cans to bulk milk straight trucks and semis, **1**, to panel trucks and delivery vans that carry packaged milk and products to homes and retailers.

A tractor pulling a milk tank trailer crosses New York, Ontario & Western tracks at Middletown, N.Y., shortly before the railroad shut down in 1957. The photo is symbolic of the milk traffic that once traveled mainly by rail (the O&W was once New York City's largest milk supplier) and had, by that date, mostly gone to the highway.
Jim Shaughnessy

Horse-drawn wagons were farmers' only early options for getting milk to creameries and collection stations into the 1900s. Neighboring farmers often shared this duty. *Jeff Wilson collection*

Horse-drawn wagons were used to make deliveries to households in cities. This service extended quite late in some areas—this is Syracuse, N.Y., in 1941. *John Collier, Library of Congress*

Body styles varied, but the most-common can truck from the 1930s through the 1960s was an enclosed body with doors on each side and rear. The rounded front and rear roofs were common. *Jeff Wilson collection*

Although not directly related to railroads, they provided a vital early link between farmers and creameries and—in many cities—from milk platforms to processing plants. They're found around creameries and in towns and along highways, and represent distinctive details that are worth modeling. Understanding the various types of trucks used for dairy operations will help ensure more accurate models.

Wagons

When the dairy industry first developed to a point of making products for wider distribution, the horse-drawn wagon was the only non-railroad option for transport. Creameries and collection stations were numerous into the early 1900s to ensure that farmers could make a round-trip to deliver milk and cream in a reasonable amount of time—four or five miles was a typical maximum distance, **2**.

Wagons were used for home-delivery milk routes in towns and large cities alike. Horses were smarter than trucks: An advantage of a horse-drawn wagon is that the driver would be able to grab a case or two, and as he made his delivery to multiple houses along a street, the horse would keep pace, walking forward to the next off-loading point.

Although in some areas this service extended quite late, **3**, by the 1910s and '20s, delivery trucks were taking over much of this delivery service. Horses were expensive to maintain, and as city dairies grew in size, substantial space and expense was needed for barns to hold horses, along with feed and upkeep (blacksmithing, harnesses, bedding, manure cleanup, veterinary care, etc.). Horses must be fed and cared for whether or not they are on duty, unlike a truck, which doesn't need fuel until it is started.

Speed was another factor as trucks took over. Although this wasn't as critical for milk delivery routes, increased speed and capacity made a big difference in getting milk from farms to creameries. Truck routes could now extend far beyond the few miles of a horse-and-wagon run.

5

A creamery worker shovels chunks of ice atop two layers of cans in a can truck at Enosburg Falls, Vt., in 1941. The truck had just been loaded for a shipment for another creamery. *Jack Delano, Library of Congress*

6

Open-rack trucks were also used for milk. This one had a capacity of 98 cans (about 5½ tons loaded), plus it pulled a trailer (out of frame to the right). Note the tarps used to shield cans from sunlight. *Russell Lee, Library of Congress*

Can trucks

As creameries became larger (and roads became better, and trucks became bigger), most of them established milk routes with can trucks to pick up milk from multiple farms, **4**. These can trucks went on their routes in the morning, bringing in cans from the morning and previous evening's milkings. Most were very basic, with a simple box body with doors on each side and the rear. Inside they could hold two layers of cans, with chains or other restraining devices to keep cans in place. They were not refrigerated, as the cans would not be aboard for more than an hour or two.

These trucks were also used to transfer milk among creameries (sometimes to bring milk from collection creameries to city processing plants) prior to the coming of bulk milk trucks. As with railroad can cars, ice could be shoveled atop loads for longer trips, **5**. These trucks would NOT be used for transporting finished milk products.

There were other styles of can trucks as well, including some with open construction, **6**. In addition, farm trucks were often used to bring milk to creameries as well, **7**.

Bulk trucks

As with railcars, the efficiencies of being able to carry milk in bulk in large tanks had many advantages over cans. The first bulk milk trucks

7

Farmers often used their standard trucks to deliver milk, as here at East Berkshire, Vt. A rope tied across the rear secures the cans; note the rolled-up tarp or blanket at the front to cover them and block the sun. *Jack Delano, Library of Congress*

8

Heil built the first stainless-steel bulk milk truck in 1927. This 3,500-gallon tank has 2½ inches of insulation between the inner and outer layers of steel. It rides on a Federal truck chassis. *Heil Co.*

This tractor and single-axle stainless-steel bulk trailer were hauling milk in Chicago in the 1940s. *Jeff Wilson collection*

Trucks began replacing wagons for home delivery by the 1910s. This Hilltop Farms Dairy truck was placed in service in Washington, D.C., in 1925. *Library of Congress*

Dairy home-delivery trucks were simple, with an open area in the rear for cases of milk, cream, cottage cheese, and other products. They were not refrigerated. This is in San Angelo, Texas, in 1939. *Russell Lee, Library of Congress*

appeared in the 1910s, but stainless-steel tanks made them more practical by the late 1920s **8** They became popular for delivering milk from collection creameries to city milk plants. In the late 1930s, farms began switching from cans to bulk tanks, and bulk straight trucks became the method of picking up milk daily.

Trailers soon followed, **9**. As Chapter 4 explained, railroads in the mid-1930s briefly experimented with carrying tank trailers in piggyback service for milk, but the operation was not efficient enough to be worthwhile. Most milk tractor-trailers were used for large-scale transport among creameries, and their increasing size and efficiency were what eventually doomed rail tank cars in the 1950s and 1960s.

Delivery trucks

Home delivery of milk and milk products began in the late 1800s, beginning largely because retail stores didn't have refrigeration equipment and coolers that allowed storing products for sale. Dairies had fleets of wagons, then trucks, that would deliver products daily to homes and routes throughout a town or city, **10**.

The trucks would load at the dairy in the early morning hours, each with a set route of households. The driver made his rounds starting before dawn, going house-to-house picking up empty bottles left out, often with a note of what was needed that day. The milk was sometimes simply left on the porch or a step, but many houses of that period had a milk door near the main door. This small door opened to a compartment that had another door opened from the inside, and protected the milk from the sun (not to mention any stray dogs or cats). Drivers would finish their routes in late morning and return empties to the dairy.

As delivery trucks evolved, they became enclosed, usually with sliding or bi-fold side doors and rear hinged doors. They were open in the back. Cases of milk bottles and other products were stacked, and the driver would pull them as necessary in making deliveries, **11**.

These trucks were typically not refrigerated, but in warm weather ice could be placed atop the load in the back, covered by a large tarp or insulated blanket.

Electric trucks were common in big cities through the 1940s. Their chief limitation was speed, which was not a major concern for city delivery service. Walker, **12**, was a major manufacturer, and offered several models (and capacities) of its distinctive, square-bodied vehicles from 1907 until 1942. Other manufacturers included Ward and the Detroit Electric Vehicle Co.

Most major truck manufacturers also made delivery trucks or panel trucks used by dairy companies, including Ford, GMC (the "Creamliner"), and Chevy, with bodies from many manufacturers.

Divco trucks (built by the Detroit Industrial Vehicle Co.), **13**, were *the* iconic milk delivery truck, and were built in many sizes and variations from 1927 to 1986. The familiar snub-nosed, curved-hood "Model U" version first appeared in 1937 and didn't change much until 1986. These were identified most heavily with milk, but were used by other delivery services as well, such as bakeries and laundries.

A step up from the home delivery truck was the wholesale or retail delivery truck. These were full-size straight trucks with insulated and later refrigerated bodies, used to bring multiple cases of products to retailers and restaurants, **14**. The refrigerated trailer, which became common in the 1950s, was used to bring large loads between dairies and wholesalers. The larger trailers (40-footers by the late 1950s) took much of the finished-product traffic (butter, cheese, and others) from railroads.

Electric vehicles were popular as city delivery trucks into the 1940s. This Supplee truck is at Bryn Mawr, Pa., in 1943, highlighting the female driver during World War. *John Vachon, Library of Congress*

Divco trucks were popular for home-delivery companies, especially dairies. This basic body style with distinctive rounded nose was built starting in 1937; this truck is shown in 1953. *Jeff Wilson collection*

Larger trucks were used to deliver milk products to retailers, restaurants, and other business customers. This Dodge truck with refrigerated body is shown in Baltimore, Md., in 1943. *Marjory Collins, Library of Congress*

Bibliography

Books

Celebrating Tradition, Building the Future: 75 Years of Land O' Lakes. Land O' Lakes Inc., 1996

The Delaware, Lackawanna & Western Railroad in the Twentieth Century, by Thomas Townsend Taber. Thomas Townsend Taber, 1980

Merchants Despatch: Its History and Equipment, by Roger C. Hinman. Signature Press, 2011

Milk: A Local and Global History, by Deborah Valenze. Yale University Press, 2011

Milk: The Surprising Story of Milk Through the Ages, by Anne Mendelson. Alfred A. Knopf, a division of Random House, 2008

Milk Money, by Kirk Kardashian. University of New Hampshire Press, 2012

New York Central Railroad, by Brian Solomon with Mike Schafer. Voyageur Press, an imprint of MBI Publishing Co., 2007

New York, Ontario & Western Railway: Milk Cans, Mixed Trains, and Motor Cars, by Robert E. Mohowski. Garrigues House, 1995

Organization of the Butter and Cheese Industries, by Roy C. Potts. The American Institute of Agriculture, 1922

Railway Milk Cars, Volumes 1 and 2, by Robert A. Liljestrand and John Nehrich; *Railway Milk Cars, Volumes 3 and 4,* by Robert R. Bahrs.

The Rutland Road, Second Edition, by Jim Shaughnessy. Syracuse University Press, 1997.

Where Have All the Cheese Factories Gone? Advantage Printing, 2009

Periodicals

"Baltimore & Ohio Railroad Milk Cars," *The Sentinel* (Baltimore & Ohio Historical Society), July/August 1991, p. 5.

"Bennington County Co-operative Creamery, Manchester Depot, Vermont," by Warren Dodgson, Rutland Railroad Historical Society *Newsliner,* Summer 1992, p. 17.

"Borden's Milk Tank Car," by George Dutka, Rutland Railroad Historical Society *Newsliner,* March 1989, p. 26.

"Bottling Milk," by Bob Mohowski, *Railroad Model Craftsman,* March 1986, p. 115.

"The C&NW's Milk Cars," by Joe Follmar, *North Western Lines* (Chicago & North Western Historical Society), Fall 1985, p. 32.

"Central Vermont Early Era Milk Cars," by George Dutka, *The Ambassador* (Central Vermont Railway Historical Society), Vol. 4, No. 2, Summer 1993, p. 22.

"Central Vermont Freight Cars in the 20th Century: Butter and Milk Cars," by Steve Horsley, *The Ambassador* (Central Vermont Railway Historical Society), Vol. 20, No. 3, p. 6.

"Central Vermont Railway Milk Cars, 530-583 Series," by George Dutka, *The Ambassador* (Central Vermont Railway Historical Society), Vol. 3, No. 2, Summer 1992, p. 7.

"Creameries in New England," by George Dutka, *The Ambassador* (Central Vermont Railway Historical Society), Vol. 2, No. 2, Summer 1991, p. 13.

"The DL&W's 42-Foot Milk Cars," by R.L. Recordon and Eric Neubauer, *Railroad Model Craftsman,* July 1991, p. 59.

"Electric Railway Freight," by William D. Middleton, *Railroad History* (Railway & Locomotive Historical Society), Autumn 1984 (Bulletin 151), p. 17.

"Erie 40-Ton Express Milk Cars," by Patrick C. Wider, *Railway Prototype Cyclopedia,* Vol. 19, p. 51.

"Erie 40-Ton Milk Car Series 6655-6699," by Walter Olevsky, *Railroad Model Craftsman,* June 1970, p. 33.

"Eric Milk and Express Car," by Harold W. Russell, *Model Railroader,* November 2014, p. 54.

"Erie's Milk/Express Cars," by Randolph R. Brown and Martin E. Obed, *The Diamond* (Erie-Lackawanna Historical Society), Vol. 26, No. 3 (2012), p. 4.

"The First Sunday Train," *The New York Times,* Aug. 12, 1900, p. 22.

"Handling Milk in Cans," by Ron Stanulevich, Rutland Railroad Historical Society *Newsliner,* Winter 2003-2004, p. 14.

"Kitbashing an Erie Milk Car," by Randolph R. Brown, *Railroad Model Craftsman,* October 1992, p. 73.

"Last Run of Milk From Randolph," by William Brigham, *The Ambassador* (Central Vermont Railway Historical Society), Vol. 16, No. 1, p. 4.

"Lehigh Valley's 'New' Milk Cars," by David G. Lambert, *Railroad Model Craftsman,* January 1993, p. 78.

"Maine Milk in the Boston Milk Shed," by Steve Pronovost, Boston & Maine Railroad Historical Society *Newsletter,* May-June 2009, p. 9.

"The Milk Business of the St. Lawrence Division," by Charles W. Brainard, New York Central System Historical Society *Headlight,* Second Quarter 2006, p. 19.

"Milk Car for the Boston & Maine," *Railway Age,* June 16, 1923, p. 1450.

"Milk Car Off-Loading," *RailModel Journal,* October 1990, p. 28.

"Milk Companies Lease Rail-Truck Units," *Railway Age,* Oct. 26, 1940, p. 602

"Milk for the Million," *North Western Lines* (Chicago & North Western Historical Society), Fall 1985, p. 28.

"Milk Operations, Part 3: Private Owner Milk Cars in the Northeast," by John Nehrich, *RailModel Journal,* January 1993, p. 33.

"Milk Operations for Modelers," Part 1: Introduction, History, and Motive Power," by John Nehrich, *RailModel Journal,* November 1991, p. 44.

"The Milk Run," by Carl A. Peterson, National Railway Historical Society *Bulletin,* Vol. 44, No. 1 (1979), p. 34.

"Milk Run: The Story of Milk Transportation by Rail," by James A.

Kindraka, National Association of S Gaugers *Dispatch,* January/February 1990, p. 17.

"Milk Shipment and Milk Cars on the Wisconsin Central and the Soo Line," by David J. Leider, *The Soo* (Soo Line Historical and Technical Society), Spring 2005, p. 6.

"Milk Train Consists," Rutland Railroad Historical Society *Newsliner,* Vol. 2, No. 4 (1988), p. 5

"The Milk Trains: Transportation of Milk in New England," Parts 1 and 2, by Robert F. Cowan, *B&M Bulletin* (Boston & Maine Railroad Historical Society), Winter 1977-1978 p. 5, Spring 1978, p. 6.

"Milk Trains, Milk Cars, and Creameries," by Chuck Yungkurth, *Railroad Model Craftsman,* June 1974, p. 26.

"Modeling the Milk Trains: Boston & Maine Combines and Milk Cars," by Bob Ellis, *RailModel Journal,* December 1991, p. 34.

"Modeling the Milk Trains, Part 1: The Midwest Milk Trains," by Robert Schleicher, *Model Railroading,* May 1986, p. 7.

"Modeling the Milk Trains, Part 1: The Midwest & East Milk Trains," by Robert Schleicher, *RailModel Journal,* August 2005, p. 10.

"Modeling the Milk Trains, Part 2: The 40-foot Pfaudler Milk Tank Cars," by Robert Schleicher, *RailModel Journal,* September 2005, p. 50.

"Modeling the Milk Trains, Part 3: The 40- and 50-Foot Wood Milk Tank Cars from Walthers HO Models," by Robert Schleicher, *RailModel Journal,* October 2005, p. 15.

"Modeling the Milk Trains, Part 6: Milk Train Operations in the Northeast," by John Nehrich, *RailModel Journal,* April 2006, p. 42.

"Modeling Soo Line 2600-Series Milk Cars," by David Leider, *Railroad Model Craftsman,* January 2007, p. 66.

"Mooving Milk by Rail," by Bert Pennypacker, *Milepost* (Friends of the Railroad Museum of Pennsylvania),

March 2005, p. 16.

"Motor Terminals Shows Rail-Highway Equipment," *Railway Age,* Vol. 107, No. 26, p. 973.

"New England Milk by Rail: 1948," by Dwight A. Smith, *B&M Bulletin* (Boston & Maine Railroad Historical Society), Vol. 26, No. 3 (2008), p. 11-17; B&M RR Historical Society *Newsletter,* May-June 2015, p. 3.

"New Lehigh Valley Milk Cars," *Railway Age,* Jan. 17, 1925, p. 229.

"New York Central Milk Car," by Walter Olevsky, *NMRA Bulletin,* July 1969, p. 16.

"Pasteurization in the Dairy Industry," by O.F. Hunziker, *The Creamery Journal,* June 1, 1916, p. 18.

"Rail-Highway Transport of Milk," *Railway Age,* Vol. 105, No. 9, p. 322.

"The Pre-War Milk Train," Rutland Railroad Historical Society *Newsliner,* March 1989, p. 23.

"Rutland Railroad's 350-Series Milk Cars," by Ralph A. Notaristefano, Rutland Railroad Historical Society *Newsliner,* Vol. 8, No. 1, Spring 1996, p. 25.

"Special Milk Cars for the Delaware & Hudson," *Railway Age,* April 11, 1902, p. 620.

"To Market by Rail: Milk Cars," by Chuck Yungkurth, *Railroad Model Craftsman,* February 1986, p. 89.

"To Market by Rail: Privately Owned Milk Cars," by Chuck Yungkurth, *Railroad Model Craftsman,* March 1986, p. 85

"To Market by Rail: Milk Containers on Flatcars," by Robert E. Mohowski, *Railroad Model Craftsman,* May 1988, p. 58.

"Whiting's Milk, WMKX—Second Section," by Steve Horsley, *The Ambassador* (Central Vermont Railway Historical Society), Vol. 18, No. 3, p. 24.

"X-Cars on the Central Vermont," by Steve Horsley, *The Ambassador* (Central Vermont Railway Historical Society), Vol. 18, No. 1, p. 14.

"The Year of the Milk Train," Rutland Railroad Historical Society *Newsliner,* April 1988, p. 4; June 1988, p. 6.

Miscellaneous

City Milk Plants: Construction and Arrangement, Bulletin No. 849, U.S. Department of Agriculture, 1920

Creamery Organization and Construction, Bulletin No. 139, Iowa State College of Agriculture, 1913

Documents of the Senate of the State of New York, January 3, 1917

The Evolution of Milk Pricing and Government Intervention in Dairy Markets, by Eric M. Erba and Andrew M. Novakovic. Paper, Cornell University Department of Agricultural, Resource, and Managerial Economics

Marketing Practices of Wisconsin and Minnesota Creameries, Bulletin No. 690, U.S. Department of Agriculture

The Milk Supply of Chicago and Washington, Bulletin 438, Bureau of Animal Industry, U.S. Department of Agriculture, 1911

Sheffield Farms Milk Plant, written historical and descriptive data, Historic American Engineering Record, National Park Service, 1991

Car and Locomotive Cyclopedia, various editions

Official Railway Equipment Register, various editions

The Creamery Journal magazine, various issues

The Dairy World magazine, various issues

Acknowledgements

Thanks to Cody Grivno, Dave Ingles, Keith Kohlmann, and John Nehrich for providing information and photos. Thanks also to all of the photographers whose work resides in the David P. Morgan Library at Kalmbach Media. Without their contributions, this book would not have been possible.

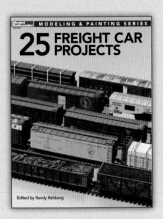
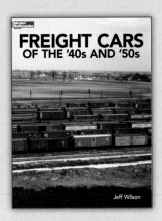
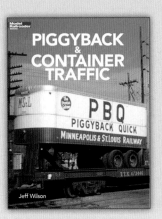
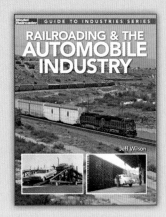